tiful
and son
Réjéan and his lovely
Mom.
May you all be
empowered for
Success.
Love
Loana.

EMPOWERED FOR SUCCESS

Create The Masterpiece Of Your Life
Using Timeless Wisdom And Powerful Principles and Techniques

LOANA MORGAN

authorHOUSE®

AuthorHouse™
1663 Liberty Drive
Bloomington, IN 47403
www.authorhouse.com
Phone: 1-800-839-8640

© 2011 Loana Morgan. All rights reserved.

No part of this book may be reproduced by any mechanical, photographic, or electronic process, or in any form of a phonographic recording nor may it be stored in a retrieval system, transmitted or otherwise be copied for public or private use – other than for "fair use" as brief quotations embodied in articles and reviews – without prior written permission of the author. Please send an email to loana.morgan@live.com for permission.

First published by AuthorHouse 2/17/2011

ISBN: 978-1-4567-3836-5 (sc)
ISBN: 978-1-4567-3837-2 (e)

Library of Congress Control Number: 2011901866

Printed in the United States of America

Any people depicted in stock imagery provided by Thinkstock are models, and such images are being used for illustrative purposes only.
Certain stock imagery © Thinkstock.

This book is printed on acid-free paper.

Because of the dynamic nature of the Internet, any web addresses or links contained in this book may have changed since publication and may no longer be valid. The views expressed in this work are solely those of the author and do not necessarily reflect the views of the publisher, and the publisher hereby disclaims any responsibility for them.

The author of this book does not dispense medical advice or prescribe the use of any techniques as a form of treatment for physical, psychological, emotional or medical problems without the advice of a physician, either directly or indirectly. The intent of the author is only to offer information of a general nature to help you in your quest for personal and professional development and well-being. This information should not replace consultation with a competent health-care professional. In the event you use any of the information in this book for yourself, which is your constitutional right, the author, her company and the publisher assume no responsibility for your actions and are in no way liable for any misuse of the information.

CONTENTS

Introduction – What Motivated Me To Write This Book xv
    Inequality in Birth and Life xv
    Equality In Conditions Does Not Guarantee Success xvii
    Driven By A Higher Calling.. xvii
    Rise Above Your Circumstances xix

Harnessing The Power Of A Magnetic Universe   1

Chapter 1.   Trinity of Luck.. 3
    Earth Luck 3
    Human Luck.. 4
    Heaven Luck 5
    How The "Trinity Of Luck" Contributes To Your Success
    And Well-Being... 6
    Do We Have Control Over Our Lives?...................................... 7

Chapter 2.   Empowered For Success 9
    What Is Your Definition Of Success?... 9
    Are We Empowered For Success? 10
    What Do You Need To Become Successful? 11

Chapter 3.   Harnessing the Power of a Magnetic Universe 13
    The Laws Of Attraction 13
    The Laws Of Attraction – Not A Magic Formula 15

Chapter 4.   Key Influences To The Laws Of Attraction 17
    Most People Live Unconscious Lives....................................... 17
    The Magnetic Influence Of Our Thoughts & Intentions 18
    The Magnetic Influence Of Our Words 19
    The Magnetic Influence Of Our Behavior and Posture.......... 20
    The Magnetic Influence Of Mass Media 21
    Television Programs And Movies..22

Chapter 5.	Cultivating Inner Qualities For Success 25
	Why Develop Your Inner Qualities For Success? 25
	Set Clear Intentions Supported With Focus 27
	Develop Patterns For Successful Thinking 28
	Make A Decision To Succeed And Commit To Yourself 28
	Monitor Your Thoughts 29
	Become Your Best Advocate And Friend............................... 30
	Your Attitudes Are The Foundations For The Greatness You Achieve. 31
	Cultivate The Right Beliefs 32
	Be Confident 34
	Be A Person Of Integrity And Character............................... 34
	Strive To Live With High Moral Virtues And Ethics............ 36
	Develop Determination And A Strong Will......................... 37
	Always Look For The Good In All That You Experience 37
	Adhere to Professional Growth Practices 37
	Don't Take Failure Personally 38
	Develop The Flexibility That You Need 38
	Develop Discipline And Consistency 39
Chapter 6.	Cultivating Habits For Success.. 41
	Be Open To Change 43
	Choose Your Company Wisely 43
	Monitor Your Habits - Are They Energy Giving Or Energy Depleting? 45
	Commit To Excellence in All That You Do 47
	Spend Time With Loved Ones 47
	Practice Goodwill.. 48
	Maintain Your Privacy 49
	Monitor The Messages You Send Out 49
	Monitor The Messages You Receive 50
	Be A Student Of Life: Embark Upon Continuous Learning. 51
	Practice The Art Of Reflection 51
	Find Time To Have Fun And Get In Touch With Your Inner Child.. 53
	Do Unto Others As You Would Have Them Do Unto You.. 53
	Practice Gratitude 54
	Moving Forward 55

Co-Creating Your Reality – Developing Your Pathway To Success   57

Chapter 7.   Self Discovery - Who Are You?...................................... 59
                 A Journey Of Self Discovery 59
                 Discover Your Life Purpose.. 61
                 Who Are You?... 61
                 Set A Clear Vision For Yourself And Live With Purpose 63
                 What Is Your Vision Of Your Life?...............................64
                 Your Vision Statement..66

Chapter 8.   What Do You Want?.. 69
                 Our Dreams And Desires..69
                 Make A List Of Everything You Want........................ 70
                 Do Not Place Limits On Your Dreams 73
                 Separate Your List Into Wants And Goals 74
                 Your Want List... 74
                 Your Goals List... 75

Chapter 9.   Convert Your Wants Into Attainable Goals................. 77
                 Goal-Setting - Making Your Dreams A Reality… 77
                 A Few Benefits Of Goal-Setting................................. 78
                 A Note For Advance Goal Setters:.............................. 79
                 Essential Strategies In Writing Goals To Get The Results You Want 79
                 Examples of Converting Your Wants Into Achievable Goals 81
                 Articulating Powerful Intentions For Goals Attainment. 84

Chapter 10.   Is This What You Really Want? 87
                 Conduct A Reality Check...88
                 Do Your Goals Align With Your Vision? 90
                 Wear Your Outcome And See If It Fits 91
                 Check The Ecology Of Your Goals............................. 92

Chapter 11.   The Power Of A Plan 95
                 Benefits Of A Plan 96

Chapter 12. Developing Your Plan For Success 101
    Select Your Top 3 to 5 Goals.. 102
    List All The Action Steps Needed.. 103
    Break Down Your Complex Steps To Achievable Ones........ 104
    Set Time Frames And Priorities 104
    What Else Is Needed To Accomplish Your Goals 105
    Take Action 107
    Review Your Progress And Practice Flexibility 108

Higher Levels of Attainment – Moving Beyond Goal Setting   111

Chapter 13. Strategies For Success 113
    Act In Alignment With Your Outcome 114
    Handling Problems And Obstacles.. 116
    Surround Yourself With Like-Minded People! 116
    Draw On Your Past Confidence.. 117
    Maintain Control Of Your Goals 117
    Your Growth Process 118

Chapter 14. Moving Beyond Traditional Strategies For Success 121
    Energize Your Goals To Make Them Compelling And Attractive... 122
    Employ Yourself At The Level Needed 123
    Know Your "Why" – Your Reasons For Pursuing Your Goals... 124
    Leveraging The Power Of Pleasure And Pain 124
    Your "Why" Should Be Bigger Than You 125
    Discover Your Why 126
    Affirmations.. 127
    Make Your Future Better Than The Past 130
    Leave Yourself Open To Greater Outcomes 131

Chapter 15. Trust in a Higher Power and a Powerfully Good Universe...133
    Many Paths To Manifesting Your Goals 134
    Maximizing The Power Of Prayer And Setting Positive Outcomes 134
    A Positive Approach To Prayer... 136
    Listen To Your Inner Messages/Intuition 138

Chapter 16. Creating The Environment For Success 141
    Electromagnetism 142
    Our Home.. 144
    What Messages Are Your Surroundings Giving About You?... 145
    Audit The Various Rooms In Your Home 146
    Clearing Old Or Negative Energy To Make Way For The New... 148
    Cleansing The Negative Energy Of A Geographical Area... 149
    How Can We Contribute To The Positive Energy................ 149
    Psychology Of Color And Your Environment 150

What We Make Of Ourselves – Creating The Masterpiece Of Your Life   155

Chapter 17. Are You Happy with What You Are Attracting and Manifesting..157
    Are You Achieving Your Outcome 157
    Use Your Intuition and Feelings As A Guide 158
    Be In Control Of What You Are Attracting........................... 158
    Maximize The Power Of Prayer And Setting Positive Outcomes 160
    Practice The Laws Of Attraction.. 160
    Implement And Practice This Book 161
    Be In A State Of Receiving... 161
    Why You May Not Receive 161
    A Few Platinum Universal Laws to Note: 163

Chapter 18. Reclaim Your Personal Power.. 165
    Social And Cultural Impact On Your Personal Power......... 168
    Let Go Of People/Relationships And Situations................... 170
    Lingering Energy Imprints From Relationships 170
    Cleansing Exercise – Cleanse Negativity From Your Relationship Field 172

Chapter 19. Managing Our Time… Managing Our Life!.................175
    Time Is Our Most Limited Resource..................................... 175
    The Importance Of Time Management................................. 177
    Preferred Style Of Time Management.................................... 177
    Creating A Consciousness On Maximizing Your Time 178
    Time Management And Life Management Tips 180

Chapter 20. Create The Masterpiece Of Your Life 187
    Design Your Vision Board To Manifest Your Goals and Dreams 187
    What Is A "Vision Board"? 187
    Why Set Up A "Vision Board"? 188
    Types Of Vision Boards 189
    Vision Boards Are Not The Same For Everyone 190
    Tips When Creating Your Board 190
    Creating And Setting Up Your Vision Board 191
    Here is an example of how to set up your board 192
    A Dream Book 194

Chapter 21. What We Make Of Ourselves 197
    As You Continue To Succeed 198
    Take Responsibilities For Your Actions 199
    Your Legacy 199
    Looking Back When We Get To The Top 200
    Be On the Lookout for Heroes 201
    The Law of Cause and Effect 201
    Everyday Is A New Day 202

*If one advances confidently in the direction of his dreams,
And endeavors to live the life which he has imagined, he will
meet with a success unexpected in common hours. He will
pass an invisible boundary; new, universal and more liberal
Laws will begin to establish themselves around and within him;
and he will live with the license of a high order of beings.
In proportion as he simplifies his life, the laws of the universe will appear less
complex…
If you have built castles in the air,
your work need not be lost; that is where they should be.
Now put the foundations under them…
Such is the character of that morrow which mere lapse
of time can never make to dawn.
Henry David Thoreau*

I DEDICATE THIS BOOK TO MY AUDIENCE...

I believe that for every book written there is an audience waiting... I dedicate this book to my audience! It is not my intention to take you along my journey, but my greatest honor to get you started on your own...

William Barclay, 20th century Scottish theologian once said that there are two great days in a person's life:

- The day they were born, and the day they discovered "why."

I would like to take it a step further and add another day:

- It is the day they look back and know that they have fulfilled that "why" and have realized their purpose here on earth!

I hope that as you read this book and work through the exercises, you will gain a greater sense of your destiny and become more aware of your personal power and enjoy a fulfilled life achieving all that you are aspiring towards.

May you be provided with the answers and guidance you are looking for, and the information that bridges the gap from where you are, to where you need to be. So that as you uncover and live your life's purpose, and discover your hidden greatness, you will know that **you are absolutely empowered for success, absolutely loved, guided and protected.**

Giving Back:

In the spirit of giving back, I am delighted to donate a portion of the sale of this book to various worldwide school building projects and other educational not for profit projects in various countries around the world.

Connect with me, I would love your feedback and to hear from you. I can be reached at:

www.loanamorgan.com

www.loanamorgan.wordpress.com

loana.morgan@live.com

Facebook Page: Empowered For Success

Facebook Group: Success Is Our Choice

For information on special corporate discounts for bulk purchases, please contact me.

INTRODUCTION

WHAT MOTIVATED ME TO WRITE THIS BOOK…

Have you ever wondered why things don't work out the way you would like? Or, have you ever wondered why becoming successful seems easier for some more than others? Why do some people seem to be "lucky" while a great majority have little or no luck at all?

What makes the difference? What makes life so fulfilling for some and not for others? What is the key to our success? Is our success some kind of a twist of fate, where our entire life is charted for us, or do we have free will? Does the answer lie in the stars, or is it to be found in using tested and proven techniques that will ultimately lead to success?

Inequality in Birth and Life

As I was growing up, I could not help but notice the socio-economic inequality that I saw throughout the world. I remember going to school with many other students whose parents could not afford many of the luxuries that others took for granted.

I saw the rich, and I saw the poor and the difference was significant and all too apparent. In many situations, I saw families who enjoyed generations of wealth and success, while other families could not afford the bare necessities of daily life. They could barely afford food for themselves and their families. These families could not provide their children with the benefit of a college or university education, and this further kept them in a cycle of lack.

In school I learnt about, and on television I saw third-world countries where there are people whose lives consist of abject poverty, disease, wars, and natural disasters. In addition, these people had no control over the weather or climatic conditions in the environment they lived in and these caused further hardships.

These observations troubled me deeply that these people had to endure such terrible suffering through no fault of their own but as a seemingly unavoidable consequence of the place and conditions under which they were born. Like many others, I came to question "Why it is that every human being is not given an equal chance in life?"

In addition, I could not ignore the disequilibrium in life as a result of inequalities in birth and place. I came to realize that the place of birth for many could either create or destroy their chances of success. Let's face it, as we look around the world, there are people who are born into societies where there is so much poverty and lack that there is little choice when it comes to survival.

On the other hand, there are countries where people are born into abundance. These people are provided with far more than the basic necessities of life and have free reign in exercising their God-given free will! Yet, under adverse conditions and humble upbringings, and with no generational history, some people living under both conditions grew to achieve great successes in life.

I saw wealthy nations where there was abundance all around and people had a choice and the financial means to provide the best for themselves and their families.

When I noticed this disequilibrium, I concluded that success was not solely dependent 100 percent on human effort! There had to be more to it. There must have been other factors involved because if people could depend 100 percent on human effort then everyone would have the opportunity to pull themselves out of poverty and provide the best life for themselves.

I also met people who knew that they had what it took to succeed but lacked the skills needed to move them forward. What about you? Do you know someone who has the gift that, "everything he or she touches turns to gold"? Or do you know people who tried everything yet never seemed to get the big breaks they were looking for?

With this in mind, I went in search of some answers - to find ways to empower people to recognize that in this age of enlightenment we have all that we need in order to move us out of the depths of mediocrity and suffering and into the heights of success. I knew that human beings are capable of so much more in life and can make a difference in their lives and the lives of the others and the world around them.

Equality In Conditions Does Not Guarantee Success

As I grew older, I became part of the working world and also owned several businesses. During that time, I noticed that there were many people who established similar businesses in various industries, under the same conditions, and in the same areas, yet there were few who succeeded and even fewer who made it to the top. I encountered people who worked exceedingly hard and carefully exercised strategies for success, and still found it difficult or sometimes impossible to achieve their goals. Many eventually gave up or settled for much less than they had wanted.

I became involved in the motivational and self-help industry where I observed similar results. There were thousands of people reading motivational and self-help books and going to coaching programs. People who were practicing affirmations, writing goals, faithfully envisioning and practicing various success strategies and exercises, and yet years later found that their results fell short of their expectations, while a chosen few made it big.

Then I became a Coach myself, and while involved in the coaching and motivational/self-help industries for several years, those observations continued to intrigue me. After years of observing people, I could not ignore what I saw around me - many people were doing everything they were taught to do and following what appeared to be the perfect plan and yet were not getting the breakthroughs they were seeking.

I knew something was missing. I had observed many of my friends and associates participating in various programs that produced results for other people but not for them. In many instances, the vast majority were still left to wonder how to grow to the next level of success.

Driven By A Higher Calling

I was always driven by a higher calling and a deeper passion. I was moved by all the suffering that I saw existing in the world and I wanted to make a difference. Since God created us in His/Her divine image, I felt great suffering could be eliminated if we all recognize and acknowledge the power that exists in each of us.

There was always a part of me that was motivated to create a better life for mankind in this world. I had always recognized the vast potential that lies in each of us. As I looked around and saw a world that was filled with so much abundance, I noticed there were so many who were living in "lack" and not realizing their true potential. Looking back I was always a student of life and success, not the kind of success that the world speaks about, but the individualistic type of success that fills a hunger inside each of us - the hunger that drives us to fulfill the destiny that we are meant to actualize.

I took my observations to a new level and started to study the lives of successful men and women. I started to observe the lives of motivational speakers, self-help gurus, coaches, psychics, astrologers, and pastors to see if they had the answers! I studied some of the best coaches and motivational speakers such as Tony Robbins, Jim Rohn, Brian Tracy, Zig Ziglar, Joel Osteen, John Maxwell, Donald Trump and Les Brown. I even studied "The Secret" and "Law of Attraction."

I believe that we are all empowered for success and success does not have to be for a chosen few and is not limited by our family background, status in life, or place of birth. My core focus was to discover how anyone could be successful and fulfill their God-given destiny no matter what their background or status in life. Success leaves clues and I was focussed on finding them.

I was fortunate that during my search, I stumbled upon an article that really helped put everything together for me. It was based on ancient Chinese wisdom that indicated that our life is greatly influenced by a few important factors that govern our successes and the most influential areas of our lives. They referred to this as the "Trinity of Luck".

This was my "aha" moment that really resonated with me, and I felt that after numerous years of searching I had finally found the missing part of what I was looking for. I knew that for the first time I had found a theory that made sense to me and provided answers to the many questions I had. It provided ancient wisdom that is still applicable in a modern era!

I have found that each segment of that theory can be applied to the different areas of our lives, especially with success and so-called "luck". I am very happy to say that I have introduced it in my first chapter and incorporated in the framework of this book.

Rise Above Your Circumstances

Very often, I hear people say that we can have anything that we want. I believe that we all were born with a specific blueprint, and like pieces of a puzzle, we have a unique role to play in this life. We are all given our unique gifts and abilities and it should be our focus to discover what those special gifts and abilities are.

We are all born into different circumstances in life, and it is our responsibility to live the best life we can and make the most of every opportunity that we are given. If you are born into circumstances that are not what you would like, then, rise above them and cultivate the attitude, mindset, habits and qualities that are needed in order to create the life that you desire.

Contrary to what you may have been taught there is nothing frivolous or superficial about pursuing what you want. Getting what you want isn't a luxury that can wait until you've taken care of all the "serious" or "urgent" life issues that are vying for your attention. It is a necessity, since sometimes what you want is really what's needed to take you to the next level!

Most people are never taught techniques to make their dreams a reality. They are never taught that it is possible to achieve their deepest lifelong dreams and visions. It is sad, but I believe that many people leave this world without ever fully realizing all that they were capable of achieving.

Whatever your individual dreams and goals may be, whether they are modest or magnanimous, there is a higher purpose for it. Your core focus is to *"begin now"* to bring it into fruition.

In this book, I have given you ageless information and a variety of techniques for accelerated results in the shortest possible time, yet facilitating all the richness that is derived from personal development and the growth that is acquired as a result. I have provided highly effective techniques and strategies that you can implement in order to improve your chances for success and increase your personal power to take you to higher levels of development than ever before.

Your dearest desire comes from your core and you are provided with all that you need in order to make it a reality. So honor yourself and let your life be different, make it a reality and the time to start is now! So with that in mind, let's begin… ☺

HARNESSING THE POWER OF A MAGNETIC UNIVERSE

Your time is limited, so don't waste it living someone else's life.
Don't be trapped by dogma – which is living the results of other people's thinking.
Don't let the noise of other's opinions drown out your own inner voice.
And most importantly, have the courage to follow your heart and intuition.
They somehow already know what you truly want to become.
Everything else is secondary.
Steve Jobs Apple Co-Founder

CHAPTER 1

To let life happen to you is irresponsible
To create your day is your divine right
Ramtha

TRINITY OF LUCK

Ancient Chinese philosophy states that humankind's well-being is not only determined by their own free will and efforts, but also by the energetic influences of the heavens and the earth. In a nutshell, it states that our life is greatly influenced by three factors: Human Luck, Earth Luck, and Heaven Luck.

We need to become aware of these influences in our lives, and learn how to align ourselves with the factors that rule and govern success and the natural order of the universe we live in. In doing so, we will be able to benefit from a vast amount of good fortune, luck, and success throughout our lives.

So what exactly are these three factors and how do they contribute to your success and well being?

Earth Luck

Earth Luck is comprised of environmental influences, such as our homes and work environments and the cities and countries in which we live. The odds of success are initially greater for someone born in a country of freedom and wealth than for someone who is born into a poverty-stricken family or country.

We all live in this multi-dimensional environment. Therefore this Earth Luck concerns the balance and harmony between ourselves and all that surrounds us. It reflects the way we orient ourselves in order to tap into the many positive energies and opportunities around us.

Human beings are a magnetic field operating within a larger electromagnetic field - the earth. When we are correctly aligned with our surroundings, we are able to flow in harmony with all that we are aspiring towards, our relationships, and the successes we are hoping for.

Our surroundings are constantly communicating unconscious messages to the universe, twenty-four hours a day. We can attract happiness, success, and wealth with our efforts, but if our surroundings do not convey that message, then the results will not match what we hope to achieve.

All of us should consciously try to align our surroundings with all that we are aspiring towards. (I have gone into more details on this subject in Chapter 16 on "Creating the Environment for Success").

As we become consciously aware of these factors and improve our environment, we will start to think, feel, and act in a manner consistent with the life we have always envisioned for ourselves.

Human Luck

We have the ability to attract and achieve what we want in life and to enhance our magnetism within this universal magnetic field. Our Human Luck refers to everything we create through our own efforts and is the kind of luck we develop during the course of our lifetime. This luck, and our ability to develop into the person we would like to become, is directly related to the skills, talents, and abilities that we increase and enhance in ourselves.

It is essentially the luck, good fortune, and success that we create for ourselves by our own actions and the decisions that we make. This is the part of our life over which we have 100 percent control. It is achieved and developed through our up-bringing, virtues, education, our own actions and decisions, life strategies, and our willingness to work hard and intelligently in order to attain our goals.

We can directly influence our ability to become successful and gain happiness by acquiring skills, talents, and abilities for ourselves during the course of our lifetime.

Human Luck is also the result of exploring our world and trying to better ourselves by growing as human beings and involves all that we do in order to expand and create our inner world through our own thoughts and our ideas.

We increase this luck through the knowledge and experience we gain from business, our career, our life experiences and the relationships with others, exploring the world, personal and professional training and by effectively navigating our chosen path using the best strategies and techniques. This is the luck that most motivational speakers and self-help authors write about.

Heaven Luck

Heaven Luck is the luck that followed us when we came to this earth. Some people refer to this as your "destiny". Others refer to it as "Karma". You cannot deny the fact that you had no say as to the place and time of your birth, or whether you were born into a rich family or a poor one, your status in life or your physical appearance.

Many people believe that this type of luck does not depend on us and that we can do nothing to change it. However, ***I believe that we can do something to change it.***

This aspect of our lives is greatly affected by the laws of cause and effect. This law (in a nutshell) states that all the good that we do will come back to us in one form or another and that the reverse takes place when our negative actions result in negative consequences in our life.

Therefore, this is the type of luck that we create for ourselves not just for the present but also for the future. It is our mode of operating in various situations in life. We achieve this kind of luck through the good deeds that we do, the way that we interact with every being that we meet, and the positive impact that we create to foster the wellbeing of others.

Many cultures believe that the power of good deeds, positive intentions, prayers, and fasting can elevate us to improve our luck in this life and beyond. I would relate this luck as having an effect on the well-being of your soul.

God gave us free will so that we can design our lives. We contribute to the shaping of our own destiny by the everyday decisions and deeds that may either bring us good "Karma" or bad "Karma". ***We cannot change the past, but we can consciously change our present and our future.*** Towards the end of our lives, as we look back, we will determine how we have used the beautiful energy and life that we were blessed with and the results we produced whether good or bad.

How The "Trinity Of Luck" Contributes To Your Success And Well-Being

You may not have had a conscious choice in where you were born or the home you were born into or your status in life. But guess what? You have been given the free will to change your destiny and co-create the life that you have always dreamed about. What will give you the added advantage, is to know the factors that affect you when developing the strategies that navigate your life into what you would like it to be.

The journey of success in life is not based on the cards you are dealt, but on how well you play and know the rules, tips, tricks and techniques. Since we are made up of mind, body, spirit, and soul; success and luck are created by many different factors - some more obvious than others. Therefore, when grooming ourselves for success and happiness, we need to address all those areas of our lives. The theory of the 'Trinity of Luck' provides a framework that covers all of them.

With this in mind, from start to finish this book incorporates a variety of strategies and information that can enhance our Human, Earth, and Heaven Luck, thereby enriching and adding value to our minds, bodies, spirits, and souls.

I have seen many books and coaching programs that are written for success that cater to one or two aspects of who we are - namely our "mind and body" or "spirit and soul". But I have seen very few that cater to all. In this book, I have incorporated information for success in all four areas. It is fashioned around blending timeless wisdom with modern techniques and strategies to propel you forward to fulfilling the destiny you were created for.

During this process of enhancement, all that we accomplish will positively impact our physical, spiritual, and mental world and provide us with greater success and fulfillment. We will be able to assist as co-creators of our reality and move beyond this material world enjoying the kind of success that truly fulfills our destiny and purpose here on earth. Our successes will remain long after we have moved on from this world.

The key to the "Trinity of Luck" is to live a balanced life by incorporating effective strategies in all the areas of influence in our lives. We can shape our destiny and create the life and success that we are aspiring towards.

I believe that in order to truly live a fulfilled life and gain lasting success and become wiser and more evolved in this life, we need to develop and nurture those four aspects of who we are.

Do We Have Control Over Our Lives?

We have far more control over our lives than most people think. Our focus should be on learning to harness our personal power and our natural talents, combined with the resources we have been given, so that we will be capable of handling anything that comes our way!

When God gives us a dream in our hearts, He also gives us the abilities and resources to fulfill that dream. We are co-creators of our reality and are responsible for creating the life that we would like to live. In the words of Billy Mill, "every passion has its destiny."

It is now time to realize that in order to break those patterns that we dislike, and take control of our lives and our actions, and create a vision that is consistent with all that we would like for ourselves, we need to find new workable strategies for success.

Most importantly, believe in yourself. If you are not happy with some area of success in your life, every day is a new day and you are faced with several choices. Even if they do not seem apparent to you at that time, you can change your life and create the one life that you are seeking.

I have provided various concepts and some advance achievement strategies that anyone can implement in order to discover what their life's purpose is and then be able to develop a plan to achieve their goals.

As you read this book and practice all that it offers, you will be empowered to enrich and add value to your mind, body, spirit and soul and in doing so ***create the masterpiece of your life by:***

- Understanding and harnessing the power of a magnetic universe

- Develop qualities that are needed to attract higher levels of success and live an ethically driven life

- Cultivate habits to attract success

- Uncover your purpose here on earth, if you haven't already done so

- Move beyond "wishing" and towards achieving your life and business goals

- Maximize the power of prayer and positive intentions to your advantage

- Develop your plan for success and design a life individually tailored for you

- Release what no longer serves you

- Crystallize your plans and strategies for success

- Move into higher levels of goal attainment

By all means this is not the "end all" but is hopefully the beginning or continuation (depending on where you are) of your success journey. Success in life and with your goals are not only measured by the size of your bankbook or your assets but can be reflected in so many ways.

When you improve how you think, feel, and act you will greatly improve your chances for success. When you increase your chances for success, you will improve your ability to be happy, to learn and to grow, and to make a more significant contribution to this world. In doing this, you will as a result contribute to the growth and development of your soul.

So with that in mind let us begin your journey…

CHAPTER 2

The greatest danger for most of us is not that our aim is too high and we miss it,
But that it is too low and we reach it…
Michelangelo

EMPOWERED FOR SUCCESS

What Is Your Definition Of Success?

"Success" can be subjective: each of us has our own interpretation of what it means because we are endowed with our unique abilities and aspirations. If I were to ask you what your interpretation of success was, it may be vastly different from how others view it. Chances are, the majority of you would come up with different versions of what success means to you.

For some people, having success is raising the best family, making this world a better place, or finding their "soul mate". Having true success in life is not only about all the material possessions that they acquire, but also about the person they become in the process.

For others, success may mean taking their careers to the highest level, or establishing a million-dollar company, or exceeding their business goals and objectives and having all the material things that money can buy.

Success can be a combination of all of the above, and we do not need to have one at the expense of the other. We can acquire financial security and wealth and make a positive contribution to the people around us and in the world. (It does not matter the size of our positive contribution as much as it is our intentions and the capabilities you are equipped with.)

The fact is that having success means multiple things to different people and can be contextual, based on what we are seeking in life and in business.

One of the best definitions of success I have come across is this, "Success is simply realizing the attainment of a goal or a dream that your heart is deeply connected to". It is the birthing of a dream that fuels passion and drive inside of you and gives you a hunger you simply cannot deny".

As human beings, we are here to experience as much as possible and to grow as souls evolving through this great cosmos we occupy in time. If we truly want to be successful in life and live a fulfilled destiny, then success will come when we incorporate the right strategies and techniques and an effective game plan.

When we recognize the divinity we are born with, our own set of special abilities, strengths, and weaknesses, we will discover that we are equipped with everything that we need to fulfill our purpose here on earth.

We all have our unique purpose here on earth - a special one that only we were created for. We are like pieces of a big jigsaw puzzle, and when put together we create an absolutely beautiful picture - the masterpiece of all masterpieces.

At the end of our life's journey, we leave behind the legacy we have built, and we take with us all that we have learned and all the good we have accomplished. Whether it lies in the lives of people we have touched, or the projects we have been a part of, we should always aspire to leave this world a far better place than we found it.

Are We Empowered For Success?

I have spent most of my life observing people around me who have tremendous potential and personal power, yet they lacked belief in themselves. Some were either held back by people who were afraid of their greatness and managed to make them feel insecure and insignificant: while others knew their own worth but lacked the skills needed to move themselves forward.

It's so easy to look at others who appear more successful than us and compare ourselves unfavorably to them or to want what they have. At other times, we may look at ourselves in the face of adversity; or compare our own successes and wonder who are we, to walk in such greatness: and may have a tendency to minimize our own capabilities and our God given rights to greatness.

I know that each of us can achieve things far beyond our wildest imaginations in areas of life we have yet to explore. I know this because throughout my life

I have witnessed what happens to people when they finally discover their vast resources, potential, special abilities, and power.

We are all masterpieces, sculpted and carefully designed to be the absolute best people for the purpose for which we were created. When our Creator molded us, He/She took the time and lovingly provided the very best in each of us.

We were all given dreams and abilities that we have had since we were children (or even at birth) and in order to fulfill our unique purpose in this world, we need to know what they are. It is all too easy for us to look at others who appear to have more and to want what they have.

As we observe people around us, we begin to realize that there are many who have figured out their life's purpose and are able to use this as a guiding force. When life conditions got tough and they were faced with adversities, where others vacillated, lost ground and jumped ship, these people were able to hold steady, navigate their way and stay on course. Wouldn't it be great if we could all be like that!

What Do You Need To Become Successful?

There are literally hundreds of things that you do over and over again in order to achieve the success you are aiming for. I know that one book cannot give you all the answers to becoming successful and fulfilled in life. Volumes can be written on all the different things that contribute to the "totality" of who we are, and who we become and how to achieve success.

There is no magic formula that can work for all of us. When we are able to realize this, we will understand why numerous participants can sit at the same seminar or read the same book and yet get different messages, or be inspired for different pursuits that will lead to varying degrees of success.

As such, I am going to simplify the answers by giving some very important streamlined information that will contribute to "empowering someone for success".

I have included information for:

- someone who does not know what it is they want out of life, or what their goals and dreams are

- someone who knows what they would like out of life, but are still searching for information that they need to get themselves to success.

During the course of my life I have observed several people in leadership and other positions in various industries and have noted that even though they were at the top of their field, there were so many important qualities missing. They lacked essential qualities that are necessary in order to be truly successful from the inside out.

I have also recognized the need to stay in a peak state by implementing strategies to stay motivated and overcome any negativity. We also need to avoid the "emotional roller coaster," where one moment we are on a high and in the next, in an all time low. Therefore, I have included some very simple and effective techniques that you can implement in your life to keep you in a balanced state and in peak performance.

Time is precious and it is the most limited resource that anyone has. How we spend our time is extremely important in our journey here on earth. I have seen many friends and associates purchase books and not "get around" to completing them. For this reason, I have purposely kept this book brief, without taking away from the quality and true meaning of what it is I hope to convey.

CHAPTER 3

To whom much is given, much is expected.
Ask for what you want, but be prepared to pay for what you get." Maya Angelou

HARNESSING THE POWER OF A MAGNETIC UNIVERSE

We are electromagnetic beings surrounded by our unique force/energetic field and living within a larger electromagnetic field, the earth, and as a wider extension, our solar system and the universe. Each planet in our solar system emits its own unique frequency and magnetic influence that also has an energetic effect on the earth and its inhabitants.

When these magnetic forces are in harmony with each other our electrical impulses become stronger and our energy and vibration level increases. As a result, our thoughts get sharper and our personal magnetism is enhanced and we are able to attract positive things in our lives.

On the other hand if our magnetic forces are not in harmony with the natural forces in our environment then our electrical impulses will get weaker and it will be difficult to attract all that we are seeking to achieve. It's as though we are swimming upstream as opposed to flowing with the current.

The Laws Of Attraction

As magnetic beings operating in this magnetic universe we are able to attract the various experiences in our lives through our dominant focus. We are subject to one of the most natural laws operating in the universe called the Laws of Attraction. Simply put it is defined as "I attract to my life whatever I give my attention, energy and focus to, whether positive or negative." In other words we will attract people, events, situations, ideas and thoughts that match our dominant thoughts, words, beliefs and feelings.

If you are focused on the good and positive behaviors, intentions and outcomes in your life, you will automatically attract more good and positive things into your life. On the other hand, if you are focused upon lack and negativity, then that is what will be attracted into your life.

This Laws of Attraction does not play favorites with some and ignore others. It does not judge if what you are attracting is what you want or don't want, it simply responds to the energy or vibration of your dominant thoughts, words, beliefs, actions and intentions and would bring you more of the same.

Hence, the reason why the quality of your dominant thoughts, deeds, spoken or written words and intentions are extremely important. They can either attract the best or the worst for you. They are creating your reality. Whether you are remembering something from the past, observing something in the present, or imagining something about your future, the thought that you are focused upon in your "powerful now" activates a vibration within you. Its magnetic power reaches out into the universe and attracts people, situations and circumstances that are vibrationally similar and brings them back to you. It is like an undercurrent flowing in your life - similar to the under current in the ocean and rivers, where on the surface the water appears to be calm, but underneath it there is another force that is operating. The key to getting what you want is to harmonize your outer expressions with your inner feeling.

In the past, society has not understood these energetic influences that have been influencing the earth. And through their lack of awareness were never able to consciously utilize it for their benefit. They generally became victims, by drawing to themselves all that they did not want to attract. Most people tend to focus on the things that are painful or on the various problems in their life, instead of focusing on the solutions that could get them out of it. When we are able to focus on the solutions, we get ourselves out of the problem mode and are able to become more resourceful.

There may be times where the situation is overwhelming, where you may be going through a difficult time emotionally, mentally or health-wise and you are unable to focus on the positives or change your state, in order to bring yourself out of a depression or any negative emotions being experienced. Seek the help of your Divine Support Team. They will be able to empower or shield you and also know how to get you into a more "positive" solution-based energy and state so that you can come out victoriously.

It is also important to understand that the Laws of Attraction is already operating in your life, whether you believe that it exists or are aware of its existence. You are always in a state of creation and always have been. You are creating your reality and your future in every moment of everyday and you are doing this either consciously or subconsciously.

If you love the results you are getting in life – great. You can continue to obtain the results you are seeking, but this time you can do so with a greater level of control in manifesting exactly what it is you would like.

Fortunately in this dimension on earth things do not manifest instantaneously. There is a buffer period of time between your dominant thoughts, actions and words and the time it takes to come to fruition. This buffer of time enables you to properly evaluate your goals, aspirations and decisions and clearly decide whether they are truly what you desire.

This break also allows us the time to evaluate and not energize any unwanted thoughts that are not in our highest interest or for our greater good or can harm others. When our thoughts are in harmony with our true desires, then in most instances we are able to attract all that we are hoping for.

The Laws Of Attraction – Not A Magic Formula

I am a firm believer in the Laws of Attraction but there are a lot more to accomplishing all that you hope to achieve. Many people believe that this is all they need to do. They practice all the visualization exercises and positive thinking and then wait for the universe to deliver. But what's missing for most people is simply taking action towards the achievement of what they desire.

The Laws of Attraction is certainly not the end-all or a magic formula that will guarantee you instant results. Small issues may occasionally manifest instantly, but for larger more significant issues, *you will definitely need to apply good business sense, principles and practices and set clear intentions. You will have to take action and do the necessary work and put things into place to be able to receive what you want. There will also be challenges along the way. It is all part of your learning and growth and development as a human being along your life's journey.* Let's face it you can use the Laws of Attraction and set out running in the West trying to see a sunrise and it will not work, since the sun rises in the East.

When we are aiming for the stars with our dreams, we do need our feet firmly planted on the ground and to have a certain measure of realism about our physical and mental, learned and experienced capabilities. For example no matter how hard we try, we are not physically equipped to fly like a bird.

In addition, in order to be able to fully utilize this law in your current level of development you may sometimes need to cleanse and restructure some of your old mental, emotional, cultural, religious, psychological and in-some instances -- karmic patterns and beliefs. This may entail embarking upon a journey of self-discovery, personal and professional development and retraining. You may also need to get the help of ethical, trained professionals with a well referenced reputation to assist you.

Since you are able to attract people, situations and circumstances that are a vibrational match it is very important that you become aware of the various factors that influence what you are attracting into your life. These I will discuss in the upcoming chapter and for the remainder of this book.

CHAPTER 4

You are like a radio that can receive many stations. What you receive depends on what you pay attention to. Because you are like a radio, you can learn to set the dial and receive whatever you want to tune into.
Sanaya Roman (Personal Power Through Awareness)

KEY INFLUENCES TO THE LAWS OF ATTRACTION

Most People Live Unconscious Lives

Most people live unconscious lives, merely going through the motions without giving real thought to where their life is heading. They have no clear vision of what they would like their life to be like in one, five, ten, or fifteen years from now. They create their reality from their thoughts, feelings, and actions as they go through everyday life experiences. They are not aware that they have created exactly what they have been focusing on at an unconscious level, thus repeating the same patterns over and over again.

These people continue to live unhappy lives and may not be aware that they have choices and can break those patterns that they dislike. They can take control of their lives and create a vision that is consistent with all that they would like and find new workable strategies for success.

There are many influences to the results we are getting in our lives. By being consciously aware of them we can engage in behaviors and activities that attract all that we would like based on the vision we have for ourselves. With this awareness, we can definitely change some of the factors that attract negative results and are not consistent with what we want. Here are four everyday factors that are of significant influences in our lives:

1. The Magnetic Influence Of Our Thoughts & Intentions

As energy beings, the emotions we are experiencing and the energy behind the thoughts, words, moods or feelings we express affect our intentions and the results we are receiving. They cause us to emit vibrations that can travel through time and space, and like an invisible energy connection, these vibrations link us to our desire. The stronger our emotions - the greater the energetic pull for what it is we are hoping to achieve.

The intentions that you transmit towards others, the world and the universe at large can attract either success or failure. When you are happy and at peace, your energy is positive and it becomes easier to have control of your thoughts and emotions and to gain clarity about your life, goals, dreams and ambitions. When you are focused on something you do not want, or dislike, or are upset about, this will result in your experiencing and sending out negative energy/experiences which can lead to a lack of focus and clarity and may cause you to attract results that are contrary to what you really want.

We should always keep our thoughts pure and maintain control of our emotions. I know that there are times this can pose be a bit of a challenge - especially when you are busy and under stress or having personal problems or other issues. However, there are simple techniques that you can implement in order *to relieve stress* and be more in control of your mental and emotional state (also remember that you do have a divine support team to assist and guide you). Here are a few techniques that are easy to implement:

- Exercising or having a leisurely walk
- Yoga
- Meditation
- Finding time to relax and have fun
- Laughter
- Spending some quality alone time
- Spending quality time with loved ones
- Spending time with your pets
- Being in the presence of positive and high-vibration beings
- Spending time in prayer

Through the Laws of Attraction, like attracts like, and we need to deliberately create positive emotional states that match the feelings we will have when our goals and desires are fulfilled. We must create an energy field that will attract what we want and learn to take control of our circumstances instead of just reacting to them. Managing our emotional and mental state along with the words that we speak is so important. Our emotional and mental states along with our spoken words and actions must also be consistent with the success we are seeking.

It is always a good practice to stop and ask yourself: "What kind of thoughts am I thinking"? And "what are the emotions they are creating and sending out"?

2. The Magnetic Influence Of Our Words

The language that we use and the power of our words convey far more than just a means of communication. The energy of our language is a direct extension of our thoughts and emotional state – be it negative or positive. All words, no matter which context they are spoken in, have an energy field around them that affects the well-being of the speaker and the audience/receiver.

Our words can be projected with malice or kindness. They can imply a question or give a command, they can be direct or suggestive, they can attract or repel and they can motivate or discourage. Words can destroy or heal and can fill us with either hope and happiness or despair.

Your spoken words contribute to your conditioning and can program you for success or defeat! Always let your words work for you to produce positive results in your life. We are all the products of the words that were spoken to us as we were growing up. When repeated enough times, words can sometimes have a hypnotic effect on the recipient, if they are not aware of its effect in their life, and were not able to release and clear it. How many of you have been, or observed a child or a spouse who has been the recipient of years of verbal abuse from a loved one? What was the outcome with regard to that person's self esteem?

In verbalizing a thought you are giving life to it and bringing it into the physical realm. In order to manifest what you want, focus on and speak the things that you want. You must release confidence and conviction in the words you speak and back it up with faith, in order to emit those vibrations that will attract the best back to you.

On the flip side what negative words have you spoken about yourself that affected your self-image in an unconscious manner? I have often heard people say things like, "I could never succeed like that person" or "nothing I do amounts to much," or they say, "I always seem to attract the same loser men in life". Or "I could never do that".

Choose your words carefully and select those that are positive, motivating and uplifting. Do yourself a huge favor and "speak" health, success, prosperity, love and happiness into your life. Instead of using toxic words that destroy, learn to make positive words work for you. Learn to fill words with positive power that enhance your life and those around you. Learn to carefully plan your outcome and carefully choose your words to convey positive meanings no matter what the circumstances. Speak success, joy, abundance and happiness into your life and people around you. Become your best cheerleader and biggest fan.

3. **The Magnetic Influence Of Our Behavior and Posture**

Our Behavior

Our repeated unconscious behaviors (the way we act, react and behave) creates the energy and emotions that we feel regarding the people and situations in our life and will attract more of the same if we do not take measures to be in control of them.

For example, at various times in our lives we may be faced with negative situations and people that may try to make us feel small or do not provide the energy for us to grow and we may buy into that belief. Our behaviors tend to be consistent with our beliefs and those behaviors will create a particular type of negative energy.

If we have feelings of low self esteem and this is demonstrated in our behavior then we will tend to attract situations or people of a similar nature.

In order to get out of that situation we need to know our core self. There are times that we may not exhibit the behaviors consistent with who we truly are, but reacting to all the negatives being thrown at us.

We must always seek to center ourselves and remain true to our core values and engage in activities that will create the energy and produce the consistent behaviors for us to attract what we really want in people and situations.

One of the ways we can develop those behaviors is to cultivate the right relationships and get into the right support groups to build back the magnificent people that we are. When this is possible our life energy begins to change for the better and we will start attracting the positive behaviors that would put us on track to where we need to be.

What kind of people or situations do you want to attract? Is your behavior consistent with those people and situations? Do you want to become a top athlete? Are you demonstrating the behaviors of someone aspiring to become a top athlete? Are you in places where you can be around these people?

Our Posture

One of the keys to success is to "always act as if" you were already the person you would like to become and someone who has already achieved all that you hope for.

For example if you would like to be a highly respected person in your field, then make a list of the ideal behaviors and characteristics that person demonstrates when they are operating at their best. In writing your list be explicit and detailed regarding the behaviors and mannerisms that are needed.

Once you have completed your list, begin to emulate those qualities and actions. Emulating those qualities will not give you the skills and all that's needed to gain success, but it's a great place to start and puts you in a peak state to begin the process.

As a best practice, you must always assume the posture of the very best actions that are consistent with the vision of your ideal self. This is a very important part of the process for grooming and preparing you for the role you are aspiring to achieve.

4. The Magnetic Influence Of Mass Media

Music And Songs

Words with the addition of music is one of the greatest hypnotic stimulants and can have either a positive or negative influence on us. We tend to listen to the same music over and over and even when you believe that you are not really listening, your subconscious mind actually hears everything that is being played (and can influence your conditioning and those of your children).

As we are listening to a particular type of music and getting into the mood of the song and the singer, this will add to setting your state and the vibrations of your day.

Conducting an audit of the music that you listen to is one of the most important things you can do for yourself and your state of wellbeing.

This influence is even more applicable in situations where you are experiencing emotional highs and lows. The majority of people, when experiencing a broken heart or an emotionally low time in their life, will listen to songs that reflect the same. And as a result may add to and feed the negative experience they are going through. I have witnessed people who got into a "victim" state through the suggestive nature of some songs that led them to acts of violence or other crimes.

We all need our time to go through the healing process which does include hurt, depression, anger and so on. But in order to learn and bring yourself out in a proper manner that fosters "true growth", to attract the best that is needed, you need to get into a more positive state of mind to be able to find more applicable solutions.

What is your music telling you? Listen to the words and not the music and hear what that singer is saying to you? Are his or her words inspiring or are they filled with depression and pain? Are they trashy and filled with perversion? Are these singers spewing out their personal failures in life and relationships? Let's face it, if they have an abusive partner and want to trash them or if they hate men or women or have issues with their parents, why should we make their dirty laundry our own? Quite frankly each of us has our own life issues to deal with.

Check your feelings and energy level after you've listened to various types of music. Which ones give you the best feelings and have a positive impact on you? Make it a habit to listen to songs that inspire the best in you and empower you to be a better person in order to enjoy personal growth and inspiration to be able to deal with your own issues.

Television Programs And Movies

The same principles as music apply to television and movies, but their influence is even more powerful since all your senses are engaged auditorily, visually and kinesthetically. Monitor all that you are looking at. Is it inspiring and energizing? Are you experiencing undue fear and apprehension by exposing yourself to horrific scenes and movies projecting doom and gloom? After you have looked at a program or movie monitor the effects it had on you. Are you drained or stressed out? Are you energized or relaxed and in a positive state?

Teenagers are so readily influenced by the effects of the mass media, that the results are easy to identify. Simply look around you and you will see that the way they dress, walk and behave is usually consistent with the influence of the singers and actor/actresses in their life. I remember reading about a spiritual principle that maintains that behind every individual there are spiritual influences (be it dark forces or light forces), and that it is sometimes difficult to decipher which influence is operating behind the scenes.

It is always a good practice to analyze a movie and the intentions behind it. What is the main theme and what is the outcome? Step out of it and look at the characters in the movie. Does it make sense? Do you agree with its principles or does it conform to what is standard and normal in life? Recently, I have seen an unusual craze with some books with some unusual characters and a movie craze that had me questioning the influences behind it.

Mass media can have a powerful impact on your emotions and attract various situations into your life. It is very important for you to be aware of this and monitor what you are allowing in your consciousness. We must always be conscientious caretakers of mind, body, spirit and soul and monitor all that we program and condition ourselves with. If our intentions, thoughts, words, music and movies, our behavior and the company that we keep are not consistent with what we are hoping to achieve, then there will be a misalignment in attracting what we are hoping for. *Always ensure that they are consistent with the best for your life.*

I have seen people do the opposite, focusing and speaking things that were contrary to what they really wanted, talking about the doom and gloom of the planet and energizing what they do not want. It is so important that this be CANCELLED.

We need to be caretakers of our mind, of ourselves and of our future generations to come. Speak only the good that you want and ignore anything or anyone that is contrary to it.

CHAPTER 5

*What lies behind us, and
what lies before us, are tiny matters
compared to what lies within us…*
Ralph Waldo Emerson

CULTIVATING INNER QUALITIES FOR SUCCESS

Why Develop Your Inner Qualities For Success?

There are many things that will help you to become that person who is capable of fulfilling the path that you have chosen to pursue but very few that will actually help you develop inner fortitude and character.

Once you have decided what it is you would like to achieve, success begins with you through your inner habits and qualities and the way to exhibit yourself in all that you do, even before you have decided what it is you would like to achieve.

In fact, it is easy for us to develop a plan and follow the various key steps and gain material success in our chosen goals, but for many it's not as easy to develop the various important qualities that are needed to assist in their growth and development as a human being. How many of us have met people who are materially successful but leave much to be desired in other areas of their life. There can be a number of reasons that may have contributed to them being this way:

- They simply do not care about their impact on others

- They are ignorant through lack of awareness of their negative impact on those around them

- They are not aware of the various qualities that are needed in order to help them grow and develop as more evolved and compassionate people

- Some have found it difficult to challenge themselves to learn and incorporate new life qualities that are needed, largely because they have operated in a particular manner and style throughout most of their adult lives and have never really had a reason to change.

- And for many, personal development was never an area where they were aware that they needed to focus on and build

Our ability to gain success is based on our ability to grow as a person and is not just based on following some external step by step recipe that we must follow. In fact, we cannot separate our personal life from our career/professional life. They are integrated and have an influence and impact on each other. True success is an intimate expression of who we are at the core and is reflected in our being, our action, and our expression in the world.

People will always be a part of our lives:- in our personal relationships, in our professions and in our businesses, therefore, we must also seek to become better and gain self-mastery and develop greater people and life skills. And the place to start is to incorporate life strategies to grow and develop from the inside out. Our outer life is the direct reflection of our inner life and in order to accomplish more in life we must begin the process of developing and mastering our inner-self, our thought patterns and our conditioned habits and beliefs.

In fact, we need to also become the person who is capable of achieving all that we seek to accomplish. By growing into this person, we find ourselves in a state where we are naturally driven to accomplish the things that we have set out to do with greater flow and ease. When we look at our lives we become aware that we do not exist by ourselves. Who we are and what we do, have far reaching impact on everyone around us.

In addition, by developing and mastering the relevant skills and inner qualities needed, you are able to maintain a steady pace and develop the inner strength needed to stay motivated to attain your goals and dreams, especially when the going gets tough. It would help to build a solid foundation and resilience and these qualities that we develop in ourselves will manifest into greatness in all that we do.

There are many factors that contribute to inner success based on the individual and their stage of development in their life. These factors also depend on your perception of what you need in order to live a truly successful and fulfilling life.

In the following pages, I have provided you with a list of 16 qualities for success. This list is by no means "the end all" since there are a large number of useful qualities that one can develop. I have touched on each one of them to emphasize their importance in developing a better you. After you have read them all, if you believe that I have left out something important, please go ahead and add it to this list. Here are those qualities:

1. Set Clear Intentions Supported With Focus

Suppose you were finally going on that long overdue vacation. You have been planning and saving for it for years. Maybe it's a family vacation. You have the ticket and you're on your way to the airport. While on your way, someone calls you to come over for a barbecue. Would you turn the car around and go to the barbecue? Of course not! Not after all the sacrifice and investment you've made for that vacation along with the fact that you have done so much planning and may have had to negotiate getting the time off with your boss.

Unfortunately, in your own life you let the distractions of the moment deny you your most treasured goals – your life goals. That stops now. Rather than moving from one empty distraction to another, focus your efforts and attention toward those things that will bring true and lasting fulfillment. The payoff and benefits you will receive are priceless.

Setting your intention and controlling your focus is like a laser beam that cuts through anything stopping you. Every achieved outcome begins with a clearly focused thought about an action we want to take or something we want to produce. When our intentions are clear, then we are actually first creating the results we want in our mind before it becomes a result in our reality. We see the results in our mind's eye and then decide if this is exactly what we want.

People who are able to focus their attention and resources on the truly important goals in their lives are able to make consistent improvements in those areas - improvements that can grow exponentially with time.

That single-minded focus will allow you to shorten the time that you spend in completing whatever you are working on. It is those desires, thoughts and actions that you are putting into it that will draw what you are aspiring towards. No matter what the circumstances, keep your focus firmly planted on the outcome you are hoping to achieve. Focus on all the things that you want.

2. **Develop Patterns For Successful Thinking**

Success starts with a mindset that must begin even before you can achieve what you have set out to accomplish and before you implement all the qualities that you are seeking to develop.

In order to do this, you need to create patterns of successful thinking and successful being. When you have established an inner pattern, a particular way of being and reacting - your body and mind will naturally respond in that particular way in all situations be it negative or positive. An applicable, successful response is what will create success in all parts of your life.

You can create successful patterns by recognizing those that no longer serve you, in areas where you feel stuck. As you are able to recognize them, make a list and begin to find ways to move past them and implement new techniques for success.

One of the ways to do this is - you must begin with the perfect "end result" you are seeking. In doing so you are able to start incorporating the qualities that would draw you to those results. It is also a good practice to focus on people who have accomplished what it is you would like; then ask yourself, "What are the qualities and habits they have that I need to develop within myself in order to accomplish my goals?"

Once you have identified these qualities, begin to emulate them. In addition to these, there will be other qualities and attributes that you will have identified along the way that would serve you in a positive way by drawing you closer to your aspirations. Cultivate the qualities that boost and feed your mental, emotional, and psychological well-being.

3. **Make A Decision To Succeed And Commit To Yourself**

Every positive change in your life begins with a clear decision and a commitment that you are going to achieve your outcome, no matter what it is. Commitment is important because when you encounter an obstacle or feel as though you have "hit a wall" you will keep on moving knowing that this is your resolve and this is the path that you have chosen no matter what the circumstance.

The very first thing that you have to do in order to start becoming a success is to make a commitment to believing that nothing is going to stand in your way. Success is not just something that happens to people, it is a choice. If you study all the great leaders or some of the most successful people that you have met, you will realize that everyone in the world who is successful, at one point or another, made a very distinct decision to become that way. After they had made that decision, they explored and implemented some of the most effective strategies and disciplines that were needed in order to achieve their success. They simply did not leave it to chance or luck, or expectation only.

People who are committed and encounter difficult challenges will focus on solving those problems. People without that commitment may quit at the first sign of major problems or obstacles. These are people who were either dissatisfied with some aspect of their life, or knew that they were worth much more than the life they were living. So, they made a decision to go after success and consistently took action and persisted until they got it.

This is your life, take responsibility for the results you are getting. Commit to your success, commit to yourself. Ask yourself – Am I living the life that I want? If not, what could I do differently to begin living that life now? What could be more important for you than that? Your commitment will make things happen.

4. Monitor Your Thoughts

Everything in this world started with a single thought. Our thoughts create…

Take a look around the room. Everything you see around you was once someone else's thought. Someone had an idea, took action and followed through and was able to create their masterpiece and make their contribution to the world.

What you become, you first become in your mind. What you accomplish, is accomplished first in your mind. So what are you thinking about? Are your thoughts empowering or disempowering?

The mind is a wonderful thing with such tremendous creative potential and is bound only by the limits we place on ourselves and by our beliefs about what we think of as possibilities in our lives. Pure imagination has no boundaries or constraints. It is free as the wind. We should always give ourselves the freedom to imagine a magnificent future for ourselves.

The fact is we can literally become what we think about. You are either the captive or the captain of your thoughts.

Whatever you spend your time thinking about, you will bring into being, often unconsciously. How many times have you dreamed thoughts about something and soon after found yourself connected with that something?

Did you know that our lives today are the results of our thoughts up until now? So take mastery of your thoughts in all that you do. Your continuous thoughts leave mental and emotional impressions on yourself and assist in molding who you become. When the same thoughts are continuously energized, they begin to form your beliefs and these beliefs evoke emotions that determine the way you respond to things. They also determine your motivation and your drive to accomplish all that you have set out to do.

The quality of your life is a reflection of your thinking, the better quality of thoughts, the greater results you get.

Continuously entertaining certain thoughts create beliefs that eventually create your reality. The human mind is like a fertile ground where seeds are continually being planted – seeds of the opinions, ideas, and concepts that grow and create our reality.

Nourish your mind with a mental diet of hope, faith, confidence, gratitude, happiness, and positive thoughts. Take conscious control of your thoughts in order to create the results that you're looking for.

5. Become Your Best Advocate And Friend

As important as it is to surround yourself with the right friends and mentors, it is equally important to become our own best friend and advocate. It may not always be possible to find the right friends and mentors, so you must become the best friend and mentor that you need.

I believe that we all need to become our own best friend and learn to trust and have faith in ourselves and stand by the decisions that we have made and know to be right. There are times in this world when decisions must be made - even when no one else is involved or when others do not see your point of view. I believe that at such a moment in time you need to maintain your personal power, stay true to yourself and stand behind your decisions.

Believe in yourself and the fact that you know what is best for yourself, because - guess what? Is there really a right or a wrong dream in the pursuit of your own happiness? Why should someone have to tell you what is the best dream for you? (Unless, of course, it means harm to you or others or would interfere with someone's free will. If it does, then you have to seriously consider your decision and seek proper advice and guidance.)

We have been endowed with all the resources that we need in this life and I believe that the answers to most of our questions lie inside each of us. These answers come to us in the form of an intuition, a hunch, a thought or a feeling. Throughout our lives, there seems to be some guiding force that comes through for us when we are at that moment of decision or at various strategic times in our lives and simply guides us as we navigate our way through life. We need to start to acknowledge that there is universal love and support that exist and is waiting to guide and assist us in accomplishing our life's purpose.

Learn to love and appreciate your own self. It is so important that you become your best advocate and learn to solve your problems and create happiness for yourself. Do you know that when you continuously feel the need to turn to someone else for help, or to have them make decisions for you, you are giving away your power to that person? If you are someone who believes that you have to validate everything with someone else, you do not trust your own decision making process. It is time to start building up your self-esteem and reclaim your personal power.

Spend time with yourself to discover who you are. This can be accomplished during your private times of reflection or simply by doing the things that you enjoy.

6. Your Attitudes Are The Foundations For The Greatness You Achieve.

Do you know that you have a choice with your attitude? I have often heard that it is not what happens to you that counts – it is how you react to what happens to you that makes the difference.

Our attitudes are the established ways of responding to people and situations which we have learned. They arise from the beliefs that we have cultivated and the assumptions we hold. Your attitude dictates your behavior and as a result they also dictate your body language and the energy or vibrations that you send out at any given moment.

Cultivate and nurture a positive attitude. Your attitude creates the vibes or energy around you as you enter a room. I am sure that many of you have walked into a room and felt negative vibes being emitted from people who really put a damper on your mood, and chances are you did not want to be around them.

On the other hand, we all know people with great attitudes, people who always seem happy and positive and are fun to be around.

It is your attitude and mindset that attracts or draws the vital energy needed for happiness and success. Having a positive outlook, and the intentions to create the life that you desire - whether it is to create a home, attract a mate, improve the path of your career, or to have a healthy, happy, and wealthy life - all depends on the synergy of your attitudes, focus, and mindset.

It has been scientifically proven that maintaining a positive attitude promotes peak performance and produces chemicals that keep us healthy. On the flip side, however, a negative attitude produces negative energy and creates an imbalance in our energy system that results in ill health.

How many of us like to be around negative people? Can you imagine how others would feel to be around you, if you had a negative attitude?

Develop the attitude of always looking for possibilities on how to add value to everything you say, do, and touch, not just for your goals, dreams and ambitions, but in all areas of your life and in your relationships with others.

In order to maintain a positive healthy attitude, find the time to do things that you really enjoy. Listen to music and surround yourself with positive and uplifting images and people where ever you go. Read positive writings and try to laugh a lot, watch comedies, and spend time with loved ones. Nurture your mind, body, spirit, and soul while always enjoying whatever makes you feel happy and fulfilled.

7. Cultivate The Right Beliefs

"Belief is the key to basic mind power which turns concepts into realities."
Napoleon Hill

A belief is an assumed truth that we hold about something. It is in fact a learned truth that we acquire from our family, our friends and the culture and society that we grew up in. Most of our beliefs are absorbed from the people around us, primarily our family and friends. The power of "Belief" or "Faith", is by far one of the most *powerful and creative* force in the universe. It can be used in a way that is either negative or positive, depending on what you believe. What we believe becomes "true" since our actions arise out of our beliefs, and our actions assist in the shaping of the world we live in.

Beliefs can either be limiting or liberating. When babies are born into the world they are born free and clear, without any fears, or preconceived ideas or prejudices. As they grow up, they are shaped by the beliefs of the people around them, even if these beliefs are founded from untruths and superstitions. There are cultures that indoctrinate kids at an early age and these kids will then conform to a particular way of thinking that may not be the truth. There is a snowball effect. Fortunately as adults we do have access to information that can enlighten us so that if we open our minds we will be able to see the truth.

If we were to look at our own lives, we tend to reinforce our own beliefs by surrounding ourselves with people who share similar ones, and if not open minded enough, will stay within the confines of limited thinking. The truth is, if we let go of our limiting beliefs, we have the potential to be anything. Overcoming limiting beliefs is very important because they are usually based on fear - the type of fear that can make someone weak, and block the open energy of adopting new positive beliefs and flexibility in life.

The world is full of people who would love to destroy your beliefs about yourself and reshape your reality if you let them, but be your best fan and remember they are powerless in affecting you unless you give them permission! Constantly work on your beliefs about yourself. Constantly work on building your faith, your beliefs, and your confidence by focusing on all your dreams, goals and aspirations. Focus on all your positive traits and strengths. Listen to motivational and training tapes in your car and at home.

Listen to great music, nurture your spirit and soul, and bask in the beauty of who you are. Your belief in yourself will continue to grow as you strengthen your faith in you. Constantly bombard yourself with good stuff and surround yourself with people who love you and build your belief in who you are and what you would like to achieve.

Read autobiographies of winners and successful people who have overcome obstacles to get to where they are. Read magazines that keep you motivated and on a steady high and make you feel good about yourself.

8. Be Confident

You must be able to trust yourself and your abilities to achieve what you have set out to accomplish. To be able to trust yourself and your judgment, even while you are new at something, is one of the most important qualities in cultivating confidence.

Anyone can develop the level of confidence they need. Focus on your past achievements and develop inner qualities that will help to boost that confidence. Make it a habit to really connect with the magnificence within you and to love the person that you truly are. Your confidence will continue to develop as you focus on doing the best that you can do with the resources that you have.

Make it a point to stop comparing yourself to others and instead focus on all the progress you have made and reward yourself for it. "Celebrate you." Understand that there are no failures unless you decide to quit. Keep walking confidently in the direction of your dream.

I have found that using daily affirmations and surrounding yourself with people who love, respect, and admire you will contribute to building your self-confidence. Surround yourself with all your certificates of achievements – trophies and gifts that you love and cherish and the photographs of the people that you love and admire and who love and admire you.

9. Be A Person Of Integrity And Character

Integrity and character are two of the most important qualities that I look for in a friend or a mentor or anyone I choose to share my life with. I believe these to be two of the most important qualities we should incorporate into our everyday lifestyle. Integrity and character can mold us for greatness and position us for higher levels of respect within our circle of influence and the world at large.

All of life is lived from the inside out. At the very core of your personality lie your values about yourself and your life. Your values determine the kind of person you really are. What you believe has defined your character and your personality. It is what you stand for - and what you won't stand for - that tells you and the world the kind of person you have become. (Brian Tracy)

If you are a person of integrity, a person of quality, a person of excellence, the world will reward you with the same. This is an important key to being a winner in life and in business.

You can tell how high your level of integrity is by simply looking at the things you do in your every day life. Simply take a look at your reactions and responses to the inevitable ups and downs of life and observe the behaviors you typically engage in and you will then know the person you are.

You must be true to yourself. You must be true to the very best that is in you, to the very best that you know. Only a person who is living a life that is consistent with his or her highest values and virtues is really living a life of integrity. And when you commit to living this kind of life, you will find yourself continually raising your own standards, continually refining your definition of integrity and honesty.

You can become a superior human being by consciously acting exactly like the kind of person that you would most like to become. If you behave as an individual of high integrity and character, you will soon create within yourself the mental structure and habits of such a person. Your actions will become your reality and will create a personality that is consistent with your highest aspirations.

When you are in the company of someone with those qualities, you will find you have very few concerns regarding your dealings with them. You are never concerned that there would be any deception on their part. There is an automatic level of confidence and trust that develops when you realize that this is a person you can trust beyond the shadow of a doubt. We all need those people around us.

Always be a person who is operating with the highest and greatest intentions for others and yourself. When you take care of others, our "Creator" and the "Universe" will take care of you – a natural spin-off.

10. Strive To Live With High Moral Virtues And Ethics

The dictionary defines virtues as "having moral excellence, goodness, righteousness, and conformity of one's life and conduct to moral and ethical principles".

Have you ever met someone with high moral virtues? What impact did that person have on you and your life? Think about your leaders and the leaders around you. Would you place them in that category? More importantly, would you place yourself in that category?

As you strive towards becoming empowered for success, you will begin to realize that these are two of the most important qualities that you should practice. When you live a life of high moral virtues and ethics and strive towards creating excellence in yourself, the energy that you send out will have far reaching consequences.

We all look up to and respect people like that. We turn to them for leadership and guidance, knowing that we can rely on their word.

These qualities go hand in hand with integrity and character. When combined and lived, solid companies, families and nations are built upon those qualities.

I believe that living an ethical life filled with truth is extremely important and are qualities that transcends through time and space with you from this world into the next as you leave this earth. It is also one that affects your future since as we sow so we shall reap. When you are ethical and just to everyone, the universe is there to support you! There are universal systems in place for it.

In everything we do, we should bear in mind there are always far-reaching consequences resulting from our actions. In acknowledging this, we can choose to make decisions that contribute to the welfare of all concerned, including ourselves as opposed to choosing to service only our own needs. We must always remember that our actions have a 360-degree impact (be it negative or positive) on those around us, on the world at large, and then back to ourselves. When we choose to be in service to ourselves and the world, we contribute to the greater good - not just in the present generation but also for generations to come.

11. Develop Determination And A Strong Will

Your will and determination are like a muscle that needs exercise to get stronger. The more you exercise and push for higher levels, the stronger they become. All the great success stories are about people who encountered significant setbacks and obstacles but exercised unrelenting determination and strong will in their quest for success.

Things don't always work out the way they should and in the pursuit of our goals we may encounter obstacles and setbacks. Some may be harder than others and if you give up at the first sign of difficulty you will not achieve what you have set out to do. Keep your objectives clearly in front of you. It is at these challenging times that you must remain committed and determined to do whatever it takes in order to fulfill your goals. Continuing to persevere and persist will give you the drive, determination, and strength of will to overcome any obstacle and will mold you into becoming a person of excellence on your way to success.

12. Always Look For The Good In All That You Experience

One of the keys to success and happiness lies in the way we interpret events that unfold before us. Successful people have developed the ability to interpret negative or devastating events as challenges that will assist them in growing and moving up the ladder of success. Nothing has any real meaning except the meaning that we give it. We can either use events to empower us or to dis-empower us.

Always look for the good in all that we experience and rise above the situation you are facing and appreciate all that you are learning in the process. In most situations that you encounter, if you were to look at it at all angles; there is always some good that you can get out of it. Even if there is not – take with you all that you have learnt, by acknowledging your growth and wisdom acquired as a result of those situations. Once you have done this you can move on and not make the same mistakes.

13. Adhere to Professional Growth Practices

To reach high levels of success we need to follow personal and professional growth practices. It is the open door to all, since the major key to your better future is you.

Our ideas, beliefs, and understandings must be completely oriented toward the outcomes that we are hoping to achieve, that we must be able to eliminate any limiting beliefs and toxic thoughts that can prevent us from succeeding. Even our unconscious behaviors must be armed with essential skills needed to move us closer to our goals and skills that will enable us to not only achieve success but hold on to it.

I have continued to work on my own personal development and I must admit it is one of the most rewarding and powerful things I do for myself. These activities of personal development should last a lifetime. What you become is far more important than what you get. One of the most important questions to ask yourself on a periodical basis is, "Am I happy with the person I am becoming?"

14. Don't Take Failure Personally

Don't take failure personally but treat it as an opportunity to learn and grow. Acknowledge that failure to reach a goal does not make you a failure. Sometimes failure may simply mean that we are being prepared for our "higher" life purpose and there are many things that we need to learn along the way. These include experiences that will shape us into the person, that is capable of being a magnificent success in that role, and equip us for what God has ordained for us. Learn to adjust and grow with it, develop your flexibility and move on.

15. Develop The Flexibility That You Need

Develop flexibility, the world is changing, life is changing, and time is forever moving on. We cannot allow ourselves to stagnate in our ways of doing things or in our thinking and dealings with others. People who are adaptable and have the flexibility for change are the people who can seize opportunities as they arise. These people are successful survivors who have the ability to rise to any occasion.

History has shown us numerous situations where companies or nations were not able to adapt and either failed or were taken over. In its simplest form, many of us know someone who is difficult to get along with because they are unyielding in their ways. What were the effects in their life? And how did this affect you and the outcome of that situation?

16. Develop Discipline And Consistency

In order to achieve great success in life, you must become a special kind of person. To rise above the majority, you must develop qualities and disciplines that the average person lacks. You must be able to do the things for success that others are not willing to do. You must be willing to pay a price.

On various occasions - the beginning of a new year, the death of someone close, birthdays or at other various times in their lives, people make a decision to pursue success or achieve certain goals in their life. During that time, of decision making, when the emotions are high, they become highly motivated to pursue those goals. However, since most things that are significant and important take time to build, as time passes by they may get side tracked and burnt out and lose momentum or the motivation and drive needed to be successful. In the pursuit of our dreams, we have to consistently do the things that are needed to get done in order for us to succeed.

It has been proven over and over that the consistent investment of time and effort toward your goals and objectives will be the determining factor in your success.

One of the biggest obstacles for most people is not that they lack knowledge, but rather it is their inability to regularly act on that knowledge and to consistently take action that will inevitable produce the results they are looking for.

You will always get out of things what you put into them. Every effort that you make towards a desired task has a cumulative effect in the achievement of your goals and dreams. We should therefore choose our activities wisely and give them the priority that is required to get them done. Every activity counts.

CHAPTER 6

*Miracles start to happen when you give
as much energy to your dreams
as you do to your fears.*
Richard Wilkins

CULTIVATING HABITS FOR SUCCESS

What has manifested in our life thus far is a result of what we have allowed through our inner habits and thought patterns. By developing the right qualities and allowing them to grow and expand, we empower ourselves to develop the mindset needed to pursue our goals and we develop the ability to anticipate and rise above any challenges that will come our way.

So what is a habit? A habit is an automatic routine of behavior that we unconsciously repeat everyday without thinking. They are learned and not natural behaviors that occur automatically without any intention by the person.

Our ability to focus on and develop the right habits and to maintain our momentum will enable us to become someone who is capable of following through and accomplishing whatever we set out to accomplish.

As indicated in the previous chapter, this is not just about performing some random act of success, or following some documented recipe, that is guaranteed to bring out the greatness that lies inside each and every one of us. It is also about creating new habits that are needed to take us to the next level.

Our lives are made up of habits we have acquired over the years and almost everything we do involves the use of habitual behavior. Think about it, we have developed habits in the way we comb our hair, the way we dress, the way we communicate with people, the way we work and countless other behaviors. In fact if we did not have habits our ways of doing things would not be the same, but be completely inconsistent from day to day.

There are habits that we have cultivated that hold us back and there are habits that add value to our lives, our goals and our dreams. In fact, true success is not just the result of the correct decisions that we make, but more importantly of the habits we develop. As millions do yearly, a person may decide to go to the gym and develop a healthy lifestyle, yet how many people develop the habit to stick with it?

The key is not in the making of decisions. The key to success lies with those daily decisions that are supported by daily practices that form habits that add value to our lives. The people with the right habits are the ones who will succeed in life.

In order to accomplish your goals and dreams, you need to become a person who is capable of completing the journey along your chosen path. You need to develop the right skills, qualities and habits to attract success. When you do, you will become a magnet that will attract all that you are aspiring towards and attaining your goals will become far easier. The better you become at developing that inner person, the more consistently your efforts will produce desirable results.

You are the catalyst. You are the real deal. You are the key and are responsible for the outcome and results in your life. True and meaningful success is something that permeates every area of our life and comes not by accident, but by the deliberate choices and constructive habits that we form.

I have written down 14 habits that I have incorporated into my life and consider essential for you to add to your "toolbox of skills" for becoming a success. If you make them a part of your daily practice, they will help you to create the lifelong habits that are shared by most successful people. Being motivated is what gets you started, but cultivating the right habits is what keeps you going.

They are by no means "the end of it all," since there are so many habits that you can cultivate that will help develop a "better you". Just as with my list of qualities in the preceding chapter. If after you have read them and believe there are additional habits you would like to develop please go ahead and incorporate them!

Here they are:

1. Be Open To Change

Whether you are trying to cultivate a new habit, change an old one or incorporate new qualities, making those changes in your life may be a bit uncomfortable in the beginning. Your goal should be to develop the mindset of being open to change. However, remember that a journey of a thousand miles begins with a single step.

What will make the difference in your life is your level of commitment to your success and the development of long-term thinking. What would help with that commitment is staying focused on the benefits of the outcome you are trying to achieve. You will need to consistently practice the discipline of doing the things you have committed to do, long after the emotional high you felt at the start is gone.

Over time, as you continue to make these changes, the results will astound you. Soon you will find yourself becoming a person who is capable of living your dreams and attracting all the various opportunities for success that are there for your taking. You will find yourself unconsciously shaping your words and emulating the behaviors and characters of the people you most admire. You will take charge and be responsible for shaping your own destiny. You will find that you are no longer a victim of circumstances, but responsible for co-creating the life that you have dreamed of. Taking great control of your life is an amazing state to be in.

2. Choose Your Company Wisely

Proverbs 27:17 (New King James Version)

"As iron sharpens iron, so a man sharpens the countenance of his friend."

You cannot succeed by yourself, and even if you could, why would you want to? Sharing is great and can be so fulfilling. We get to learn from our experiences and those of others, so we can minimize our chances for failures and be better equipped to navigate our way towards success.

Sometimes it is the company we keep that hold us back through their limited thinking or their lack of skills and abilities to help you move forward. Sometimes it is their small-mindedness that is manifested through their disbelief in your goals and dreams. I remember being told by one of my mentors that unless someone has achieved what you are looking to accomplish, then you have to ask yourself, *"Why would anyone want to listen to their advice in that area?"*

Being surrounded by the right people in your life can help motivate you and keep you on a positive high. These are people you feel comfortable sharing ideas with and learning from, people who will help you to develop and grow. It is so inspiring to be able to speak to someone that you can trust and be able to share your dreams and goals openly without any fear of being judged. People who make positive contributions and are great supportive listeners are people with whom we can have fun and grow with. We all need these kinds of friends or close associates in our lives. They make the joy and successes in life twice the fun.

We have control and freedom to choose our friends and the people we spend time with. Having the right mentors and friends can definitely increase our chances for success and happiness. Associate with people who are able to compensate for your weaknesses, lack of knowledge, or limited experience. We should make a choice to surround ourselves with people who love us or people who can add value to our lives and dreams - people who believe in us and bring out the best of who we are.

I believe that there should be no stipulated preference for the social status of the perfect friend. They can come from any background, culture, age, and financial or social background. These people should have the qualities and behaviors that you admire and value or would like to develop in you or are people you love to be around, have fun with and they bring out the best in you. However, I do believe that in order to continue to grow and develop we also need to have friends or a social circle that are on our professional, spiritual, personal and philosophical level or higher. This will continue to enhance the very best in who you are and the person you would like to become.

A *mentor* is a well-respected friend and advisor who should be well-rounded and balanced, with a great deal of life and business skills to share. This should be a person of integrity who is well respected and trusted. The right mentors in your life help you circumvent the learning curve and can be a great guiding force to you. You get the benefit of sharing in their successes and failures without having to walk a similar path yourself.

Listen to what those around you are saying and evaluate whether they are the type of people you would like to have around you. Is this someone you would like to share your dreams and innermost feelings with? Are they helping you, or are they hindering your chances for success?

Associate with winners not whiners! To handle the negative situations and people in your life, simply limit your association with them or disassociate with them totally. Give yourself every chance to expand your associations with positive people.

Your life and time are too valuable to waste on people who are complaining and have uninspiring ideas or a lack of purpose and direction. Associate with winners.

3.   Monitor Your Habits - Are They Energy Giving Or Energy Depleting?

There are many different types of energy but the two I would like to focus on are your *physical energy* and your *emotional energy*. There is a high correlation between high levels of accomplishments and high levels of energy and successful people are known for having high levels of both. Taking care of your physical energy is easy – nurture and nourish your mind and body by eating the right types of food, adhering to healthy habits and getting proper sleep and exercise and you will be able to maintain high levels of physical energy.

It is your emotional energy that I would like to discuss. There are many habits that we engage in, that can either boost or deplete our emotional energy and as a result our physical energy. When we engage in habits and practices that are in harmony with- who we are and what we want and our core beliefs, it adds value to the overall greater good of our life and we feel energized and inspired.

Monitor the situations and habits that cause you to lose energy and try to avoid or eliminate those situations in your life. A simple rule is to engage in activities and associate with people who build and boost your energy and are uplifting and fun to be around.

Become aware of people, habits and situations that are energy drainers and energy stealers. Develop an awareness of how you are feeling when you are in those situations. Are they giving you energy and leaving you feeling motivated and inspired? Or do they drain your energy and leave you feeling tired and depressed?

Most people spend a tremendous amount of emotional energy on negative emotions. They focus on negative experiences that are occurring in their lives and develop habits of worry that deplete their energy levels.

Make it a regular habit to let go of all your emotional baggage. Free yourself so that you are able to move on. The truth is, we may not always be able to control the situation, but we can definitely control our reactions and the meaning that we give to it.

It is also important to forgive yourself for any mistakes you have made in the past and let them go, knowing that any day can be the first day of a new life for you. You have choices. You are not bound by any mistakes of the past. As you let go of all your mistakes, let go of all the negative emotions that accompanied them, such as - guilt, fear, humiliation, anger, sorrow, and hurt and most importantly, learn from your mistakes.

There are several techniques that can be used to release negative emotional energy and here are a few that you can implement immediately:

- Walk at least 20 to 30 minutes, three to four times a week or engage in exercise or some form of physical activity, such as cycling, yoga, running or some sporting activity that you enjoy.

- You can scream them out. Simply drive somewhere quiet and shout out everything that is frustrating you at the top of your voice, releasing it from your system.

- You can write down your mistakes and your negative habits on a piece of paper, then crumple it and throw it away or burn it with the "knowing" that you have discarded it from your life. Then list all the new habits you would like to incorporate and start doing them immediately.

- You can imagine blowing them into a colorful balloon then once it is filled with all your "stuff", you can release it and visualize it floating away taking all your mistakes and negative emotions with it. (while keeping all you have learnt)

Try them out and have fun with them and you will be surprised to see how well they work by releasing some of your burdens and freeing up your positive emotional energy.

4. Commit To Excellence in All That You Do

Throughout my life I have observed that when you commit to excellence it has a rippling effect through all aspects of your life. Excellence is achieving the highest and finest standards in whatever you are doing. I have seen people regret not having done a great job or feeling regret for not being able to do the best that they could have done, but I have never seen anyone regret committing to and delivering excellence in all that they do.

No matter what you are involved in, make a commitment to exhibit excellence in everything you do. Always ask yourself, *"Have I done my very best?"*

The pursuit of excellence is something that you do on an ongoing basis for the rest of your life. It is never "finished" – it is only complete for a particular accomplishment or aspect of your life. This level of excellence should also apply to your personal life and to your relationships with those around you.

At the end of the day or the end of your life, the excellence that you created in relationships through your various role as: friend, parent, manager, supervisor, CEO, sister or brother and so on, will have left a positive impact on the lives of everyone with whom you shared it.

This world that we live in, the time that we are allocated, the people we meet, the lives we've touched, and the impact we have made, should always be of such paramount importance that they provide us with a guiding principle for our life.

5. Spend Time With Loved Ones

Value and nurture your relationships. Put aside time for your loved ones and friends! Spend time laughing with them and nurturing your spirit and soul. Have fun with them, listen to them, and share yourself with them. Exchange ideas and dreams or just simply be you. We all need those people that we can be ourselves with, with no pretenses.

Being surrounded by your loved ones can add value to your experiences and contribute to your growth and development as a person. It can add to your reason for living and can create so much happiness for you. Encourage these people to pursue their dreams also. Take the time to catch up with what's happening in their lives. Most people get to the end of their lives and regret having spent too little quality time with their loved ones.

Sometimes we get so caught up in earning a living that we tend to forget about designing a quality of life that has balance and includes all that is special to us. Or we forget that an integral part of why we pursue success and happiness is to be able to share it with our loved ones. It does not make sense if you get to the pinnacle of success in your dreams and goals and find yourself alone.

Take time for yourself. Develop and nurture yourself. And assist those you love to build their dreams as well. Value and nurture your relationships and always allocate time for your loved ones. It's very rare that people get to the end of their lives and wish they had acquired more things! Let's face it, we leave those things behind. What is ultimately important are the lives we have touched and the difference we have made in our own domain within this world!

6. Practice Goodwill

Practice goodwill toward those with less and do not envy those with more. When we look at others who may be wealthier or more successful or in a position of power and authority we tend to want what they have or to become bitter about it. If allowed to grow, that kind of thinking breeds envy and jealousy rather than contentment. To walk in freedom, *realize that no one else can do or be what God has purposed for you!*

What can we do to break that negative habit? Practice goodwill and develop our ability to be happy for the successes of others. Whatever you give out comes back to you. If you want love then give love, and if you want to attract success then admire success in others. Most of the time, you will realize that what attracts you will be the qualities and potential that you yourself possess to one degree or the other, but it may need to be developed more. By allowing yourself to learn and grow you can also develop those same in you.

There is a price for success and most of the time we never see the sacrifices that people have made in order to reach where they are. As you begin to observe others more closely, you will realize that everyone is a teacher and you have the benefit of being a student through practice or by observation. Successful people make a tremendous amount of personal sacrifice for what they have acquired and if they have something that you want, then simply do what they do in order to get it. Practice the qualities that you admire in them including the personal sacrifice and the learning curve they went through.

As a result of your journey and experience of the past you must also remember to be generous to those who are less fortunate than you are. Practice the joy of giving. Share your knowledge and wisdom and render good advice where deserved and not necessarily needed. There are many people who want and need success but are not willing to pay the price necessary for it, while on the other hand there are people who deserve it, they have done all that is necessary and simply need some guidance and support. Give to charity or volunteer and support a cause that is greater than you. You will find that the rewards will transcend this earth and this life.

7. **Maintain Your Privacy**

I believe that many of our innermost dreams, aspirations, and plans should be kept private and be given the time needed to nurture and develop. Let's face it, not everyone may be supportive of what you are doing or even understand the choices you have made. Sometimes others may not necessarily want you to succeed.

I believe that in life there are dreams and aspirations you may share with the public and there are those that you may want to keep to yourself. These are your most intimate dreams and desires. These are the dreams that should only be shared within your "inner circle" people who have earned your trust or the right to be in your confidence. Don't allow "just anyone" in. Let them earn that right by proving to be a person of integrity in your life and by being someone who has kept their word and been a faithful and loving support along the way.

Do not allow people's self-imposed fears and limitations to affect you. Share your dreams and aspirations with those people whom you trust to fuel your desires and are your best cheerleader and supporter.

8. **Monitor The Messages You Send Out**

Do you know that there are two types of messages that you send out to the world?

The first one is the conscious message. This is conveyed through your outer expressions. It is the way you project yourself physically by the verbal messages you send out in your daily life. This is done at times when you consciously set out to communicate all that you have planned to do in any given moment, day, week, or year. It is how you communicate with others at home and at work. It is also the way you send messages via the everyday activities that you engage in as you go about your life.

The second kind of message is created on a more unconscious and inner level and has more to do with your inner self talk. These messages emanate from the way you think and feel. They are the emotions that come out in the way you react to people and situations and may be acquired habits from family members and developed habits derived and cultivated through various areas and activities that you are engaged in. This can be through the type of movies that you see, the books that you are attracted to, the music that you listen to, and the company that you keep.

We all express ourselves in both ways and whichever way is more dominant determines the energy that will be prominent in our lives. Our aim in life is to always behave and communicate in a way that is consistent with our goals and our dreams in order to be able to quickly bring them to fruition. If our outer expressions are consistent with our inner expressions, then there will be a harmonious alignment of who we are. We are "in flow" and it's as though we are flowing along the currents of our life.

9. Monitor The Messages You Receive

There are innumerable negative messages bombarding you everywhere you turn – the newspapers, television, the internet etc. Not to mention the negatives flooding in from your career or from life in general. It seems that everyone has an opinion about your life and what you are doing with it. There is a constant flow of information from friends, family, associates, the religious community etc. This information may appear to come with good intentions even though it does not always support your highest intentions or greater good.

Make it a habit to always consider whom you are receiving information from, since others may be giving advice without the benefit of relevant experience and pronouncing judgments and exercising authority when they have none. Always remember to consider everything carefully before you act on "outside" information. Weigh all the consequences before you act and if needed seek the advice of others who are trusted mentors in order to be better prepared to make wise decisions.

Remember to also maintain your poise and operate within your own wisdom and power. Inside each one of us lie the deepest truths of our lives – it is our God given guidance system, our role to uncover the truths that will guide us in our decision-making.

10. Be A Student Of Life: Embark Upon Continuous Learning

Personal growth is a journey and not a destination and in order to have more we need to become more. Personal growth occurs when you are consistently and continually learning, developing, and growing as a human being. Every experience, encounter, and challenge we face presents us with opportunities to gain knowledge, open up our points of view, expand our awareness, and learn new skills and grow.

Life only gives you what you are ready for. Opportunities pass our way every day. The question is - are we ready to seize those opportunities? We should always be a student of life and continue to grow and learn.

We should learn to recognize the experiences and life encounters that presents us with opportunities to gain knowledge, learn a new perspective, and expand and grow. What seems like obstacles and problems are sometimes there to challenge us to grow and become more so that we can move onto that next level in our evolution as a human being. Develop the skills and qualities that you need in order to support the vision you have of yourself.

Listen to inspirational materials during your journeys in the car. Make your car a library on wheels. For years, I have listened to all my motivational and coaching material in my car, and during what would normally seem like wasted time in traffic, I was able to learn and grow and stay motivated and inspired.

These tapes and books have been my constant companion, my behind-the-scenes partner in life. If you work on constantly keeping your motivation at a high level, the results will astound you. With so many things vying for our time, we really need to be conscious of how we spend it.

11. Practice The Art Of Reflection

Regularly set aside time to be quiet, to reflect. We live in a fast-paced society. From the moment we wake to the moment we go to bed, we barely have time to take a few quiet moments.

You need to know what has been accomplished so far and what needs to be done. You need to understand all the lessons you've learned in order to make way for the new and in some cases put closure to the old.

Too many times I have seen people who are still consumed with regrets and bitterness from experiences they have had and yet they claim they are moving on. They have not stopped to reflect on the past and take all they needed to learn and let go of everything they needed to release in order to grow and move on to the next experience. Are you one of those people?

Whether it is daily, weekly or monthly, we should not have to wait for a birthday, holiday, or a tragedy to occur before we start reflecting on the various aspects of our lives. After each performance, in order to analyze weaknesses and strengths, top athletes practice the art of reflection. Top executives reflect after negotiations and before any major business venture by preparing presentations and various business plans which are usually based on past performance. So if the best do it, why not treat yourself like the best and do the same? The few minutes that you take to reflect in order to analyze the various scenarios and experiences in your life, will prepare you to forge ahead confidently into the future!

Maybe you do not have regrets. Maybe you have just come out of a long-term relationship, or lost a loved one, or changed jobs, or started a new relationship. Have you taken the time to truly appreciate all that you have experienced and have you asked yourself what you have learnt from it all? Have you savored the experience? Are you still holding on to things that you should be letting go of? Have you really let go? If you experienced a personal hurt, loss, or tragedy, did you take the time to heal?

If you have just changed jobs, have you done some self-analysis to ascertain if there were things you needed to change? Were there skills that you needed to learn or patterns that you needed to alter in order to become more productive? Were there situations that you were involved in that you did not handle as effectively as you could have? If so, have you figured out how you should have handled it better?

Are you pleased with your current role? Are there things you should be doing less of? Are you happy where you are?

If it has been a while since you asked yourself these questions or if you have never done so, I strongly encourage you to take a couple of hours this week to evaluate and reflect. At the beginning of the coming month, I encourage you to see where you are and write it down. As the month progresses, you can continue to reflect and evaluate where you are going in your life.

Then, on a regular basis make it a habit to spend a few minutes every day or night in self-examination. Look at all the positives and reflect on all the negatives and try to crystallize the ideal situations in your mind. As you sleep, your mind will be able to generate various ideas and solutions to the situations you are facing. If we schedule a little time every day to be quiet and reflect, we will free our hearts and minds from the rat race of pursuing the urgent and the rushed.

Always find time for reflection and to eliminate what is no longer needed in your life. Learn to emphasize what is good and learn any necessary lessons.

12. Find Time To Have Fun And Get In Touch With Your Inner Child

Do you want to remain young and happy and revitalize your spirit and sense of playfulness? ? Would you like to be able to clear away some of your accumulated stress?

Develop a habit and spend time with friends or loved ones on a new adventure, social or sport activity, or a trip. This will keep you light-hearted and invigorated and give your mind, body, spirit, and soul a pleasurable break. You will be more creative and develop a care free spirit about life.

Be like a child again. Throw caution to the wind and have fun. Learn to let things go. If you look at a little child, they have very few cares in the world, if any. Their activities are geared towards doing all the things that they love. Every so often it's nice to do the same thing for yourself. This will assist you in maintaining peak performance and will help keep you refreshed and relaxed.

13. Do Unto Others As You Would Have Them Do Unto You

In my opinion, of all the qualities you should develop in life, "the golden rule" and do unto others as you would have them do unto you. This should be used as a guiding principle in life. I have seen so many people talk about success and all the personal qualities that someone should emulate, without mentioning that all our actions have consequences.

Yes, there are strategies to follow in order to achieve success and there are many motivational speakers who would gladly give you all the information that you need to succeed. But success is much more than using strategies. I have seen people doggedly practice and follow these guidelines and sometimes wonder why success continues to elude them. Others wonder how it is that even after they have succeeded, they are still not happy and know that something important is missing.

Treat people the way you would want to be treated. Give respect, if you want the same. Be fair to those you have dealings with in your personal and professional life. What is sent out will return to you. Almost every religion talks about this.

In all that we do, we must recognize that our actions have consequences that affect ourselves, the lives of those around us, and all the people who we come into contact with. I have seen people lose the respect of others as a result of not following this principle. I have also seen people gain respect by adhering to it.

Make it a habit to always ensure that the actions you take will have the impact on others that you would for yourself if you were in their shoes. Apply the same standards to other that you would apply to yourself.

14. Practice Gratitude

No matter where you are in life, you have come a long way. Even though at this point in your life you may not feel as though you have accomplished all that you had hoped for, be grateful that you have another day in which to make up for it. Every new day gives you another opportunity to accomplish all that our heart desires.

You have come this far in life and there are so many things to be thankful about and grateful for. Find time to have gratitude for the beautiful person you have become and learn to appreciate the journey and not just wait for the destination in order to do so. Remember, we have been given another moment in time to makeup for the time we have lost.

Life is so worth living and appreciating. With every step let us take a moment to appreciate all the beauty that is around us and all that we have accomplished. Begin to build your awareness see it and appreciate it for what it is.

Let's start with ourselves. Simply give yourself a hug and a thank you for all you have created in yourself. Each of us is a masterpiece, a work in progress. In the entire world there is only one of us. We are unique and we are special. We are loved and we are capable of so much more. God has made each one of us and blessed us with all our unique talents and abilities.

Let us take a look at our accomplishments and bask in the warmth of it all. Honor the magnificence in ourselves.

Focus on each part of your body and simply love and appreciate it. Look at your body and thank our "Creator" for the masterpiece that you are. Sing a song and laugh with yourself. Look in the mirror and smile! Do something special for yourself. Is there anything that is too much for you?

Having a feeling of gratitude is one of the highest vibrational frequencies that we can manifest. When we are truly grateful, we will automatically attract more of the same good things into our life.

Let us make it a daily habit to create a list of the things that we are grateful about! As you exercise that feeling of gratitude "Thank Yourself" and "Thank your Creator"!

Moving Forward

In order to gain success that fulfills us in all areas of our lives, we not only need to harness the power of a magnetic universe and develop our inner qualities and habit for success, we must also incorporate real techniques and strategies for success in our outer life. One of the most important tools we can implement in our lives is using the art of "Goal Setting and Goal Achievement practices".

In the next couple of chapters, we are going to work through the process of developing your goal-setting plan so you can have the edge in accomplishing all that you have set out to do. I have written the next section in such a way that:

- if you do not know what it is you want out of life, or you are uncertain about your life's purpose, you can begin to uncover it;

- if you have never written down goals for yourself you will find techniques here to get you started;

- if you know what it is you want out of life, but do not know how to achieve it, you will learn how;

- if you have already been involved in some form of goal-setting, you should be able to see what is missing for you or discover new ways to enhance or improve upon what you are doing.

CO-CREATING YOUR REALITY – DEVELOPING YOUR PATHWAY TO SUCCESS

I believe

I believe every person has within us and inexhaustible reserve of potential that we have never come close to realizing.
I believe each one of us has far more intelligence than we have ever used.
I believe each one of us is more creative than we have ever imagined.
I believe the greatest achievements of our lives lie ahead of us.
I believe that the happiest moments of our lives are yet to come.
I believe the greatest successes we will ever attain are still waiting for us on the road ahead.
I believe through learning we can solve any problems, overcome any obstacles, and achieve any goals that we have set for ourselves.
Brian Tracy

CHAPTER 7

Cherish your visions
Cherish your ideals
Cherish the music that stirs in your heart
The beauty that forms in your mind
The loveliness that drapes your purest thoughts
For out of them will grow delightful conditions
All heavenly environment
Of these if you but remain true to them
Your world would at last be built
James Allen

SELF DISCOVERY - WHO ARE YOU?

A Journey Of Self Discovery

Where are you in relation to your dreams? Are you ready for that next level in your life, in your business or in your relationships?

From experience, I have discovered that true goal-setting starts with a process of self discovery, because in order to set goals effectively you have to be able to decide what it is you truly want for yourself. You must also decide that you are not going to live someone else's life or society's expectation of who you should be.

At various stages of our lives, we need to stop and reflect on the various areas of our life and evaluate whether we are truly living the life that we would like for ourselves. In those times of reflection, we may need to re-discover who we really are; what it is we want out of life; and what it is that no longer serves us. We need to be proactive and take control of the shaping of our future by developing an effective plan that is tailored to our needs and the vision of how we would like our lives to be.

Through my years of experience and research, I have found that most people go through life in an "automatic pilot mode." They respond to situations in life instead of proactively living it and navigating it in the direction they would like to go and with the intention of the person they would like to become.

Unfortunately there are too many people who lose sight of their vision and dreams as they allow themselves to get "caught up" in contradictory activities that are not in line with their core values. They get so caught up in all the things that they feel "they have to do" and in providing for others, that they forget who they are and their purpose here on this earth.

They conform to the perceived expectations of parents, peers, loved ones and members of their profession. As time passes because of the many trials and failures they experience, some people get disillusioned and may even start to lose confidence in their own ability to achieve their dreams and they drop the bar in their expectations.

Others find themselves too busy and preoccupied with the immediate demands in their lives such as catering to family members, loved ones and careers - that they sometimes forget who they are. They forget what it is they really want and what they need in order to make themselves happy and fulfilled.

Fortunately, for many as time passes by they begin to experience a feeling of emptiness and a sense of longing to fill that space inside and they begin to question whether they are happy and what it is they really want for themselves.

On the other hand, I have seen people who set goals and failed and one of the contributing factors is that they have set abstract goals that have no real alignment with who they are and what they really want. In the pursuit of happiness before you begin any serious form of goal attainment it is important to filter out all the non-relevant "stuff" that was acquired in the past in order to accomplish what you truly want for yourself. To do this you will need to uncover and clarify:

- who you are

- your core purpose here on earth and set a clear vision for your life

- write your vision statement (should you so desire)

When you take time to work on the above you will begin to get clear on what it is you really want in all areas of your life and should you so desire, formulate your goal setting plan. This is a pivotal point on your way to fulfilling your destiny and establishing your unique presence in this world.

As you have set out on a continuous course of self discovery, all the information that you are seeking will find its way into your life. Simply trust, that our Creator and our Universal Support Team will provide all the answers and support you are seeking at the right time and in perfect order.

Discover Your Life Purpose

We are all here for a purpose and even if you are still searching for that purpose, it is not lost to you, it's just hidden somewhere within you. You simply need to retrace the stages of your life and look for all the hidden clues and missing pieces just as you would with any puzzle, in order to come up with the complete picture.

You need to discover your life purpose so that you can begin to design and live the life that you are truly meant to. In doing so, you will be able to create a life of success that is fulfilling at your very core. The kind of success that makes you jump out of bed in the morning and keeps you continuously motivated and full of energy and drive.

Your dreams, heartfelt desires and goals are like a compass in your heart, guiding you on your journey through life. It is a true vision of yourself that will drive you and create the greatest joy when you look back at the end of your life and realize that you have accomplished your goals.

This process of discovering who you are and your life purpose is a great place to start before setting your goals in the various areas of life. This understanding is essential in creating a solid foundation that is needed to accomplish all that you are aiming for. So let's begin this process by taking some time to uncover the real you.

Who Are You?

Who are you? Who is _____ (fill in your name)? How would you describe yourself to me? How would you describe yourself to the love of your life?

As you begin this exercise it is a great idea to take a journey back to when you were a child and remember all the things that you loved and were drawn to. Begin to awaken yourself to the essence of who you are and conduct a complete self analysis by answering the following questions:

- What are you naturally drawn to, fascinated by, curious about and energized by?

- What do you really love and enjoy doing?

- What are your strengths? What are you naturally good at?

- What gives you the greatest feelings of joy and satisfaction?

- What significant impact would you like to make in your family or social circle?

- When you leave this earth how would you like to be remembered? What would you like your friends and family to say about you?

- What would you like your contributions to be in this world?

There are several strategic times in our lives when our core self shines through, whether in obvious ways by our reactions to various situations and in areas where we naturally excel in or in more subtle ones that maybe manifested through our thoughts, likes, dislikes, and actions.

Each of us hold an image of the "perfect us," and in order to become that person we need to clearly outline and decide who is that person. In order to do this:

- Clearly describe the perfect image you hold of yourself. What is your image of the person you would most want to be if you had no limitations on shaping your life?

Once you have clearly written that description, evaluate your present state and ask:

- Are you currently that ideal person?

- If not, what would you need to change or become or enhance in order to become that person?

We actually begin the process of becoming that person, the moment we begin this exercise. We begin to manifest in ourselves the person we would like to become when we clarify and write down our vision of that person.

Once you have come up with the list, immediately begin to implement some of those things in your life. It is a very important concept to immediately take action. Since most people tend to put things off for later and then never seem to get around to doing it.

Set A Clear Vision For Yourself And Live With Purpose

Our personal vision statement guides us. It is the energy behind the force that navigates our life, and it unconsciously affects the decisions that we make and the path that we choose to pursue. In fact, a vision is defined as "an image of the future we seek to create." Our personal vision is one that resonates with every fiber of our being and is unique to each of us. We all need to get in touch with our inner truth in order to discover the very essence of who we are; our purpose on this earth, and the dreams and visions that are inherent within us.

We came down prepared and are all born with a vision of what we would like to manifest in this life, a vision that is linked to the destiny that we are meant to fulfill along the way. In addition, as we live our lives and are impacted by new experiences and significant events – both negative and positive, we will acquire several new visions during this life time.

For example you may have moved or visited a different country and observed negative situations such as oppression, starvation and lack of education and was so impacted that you decided to make it your cause. Or your family or friends may have gone through some devastation or personal health crisis and you may decide to be part of the group that provides a solution.

When you have discovered and are able to live your personal vision, your life takes on a whole new meaning and you are inspired to accomplish great things in the area it involves. (Your personal vision is deeply connected to your life purpose). As you begin to create your legacy and fulfill your destiny in this life you will experience an inner joy, peace, fulfillment and happiness that is beyond anything you may have experienced before.

I share the belief that when God plants a vision or a dream in our hearts, He also equips us with all the resources that we need to accomplish that vision and become the person who is capable of fulfilling it. In addition, we are absolutely supported by a divine loving universe.

As you discover who you are and identify the God given talents you have been endowed with in this life, you simply need to walk in the direction of your vision and you will begin to attract and manifest all that you need to attain success. As you continue to pursue that life purpose magical things begin to unfold. This is like the pieces of a puzzle that fit perfectly together and creates exponential success that perfectly forms what it is you have envisioned for yourself. It is as though Providence takes over, and all that you need begins to gravitate towards you!

It is so easy to identify the people who are living their life purpose. When you meet them or spend time in their presence you can feel their depth and wisdom and you know that you are in the company of greatness. This greatness could be in anyone – your mom or dad, your teacher, your CEO or manager, your friend, your coach or spiritual leader. In many instances when you meet these people you will discover that they are the ones who have overcome many great challenges and obstacles in their lives… obstacles that molded them into becoming the magnificent beings that they are!

What Is Your Vision Of Your Life?

Writing your personal vision statement is one of the first steps towards creating focus your life. If you do not have a clear vision for your life then there are many simple techniques to help you to discover it. In creating this statement of our life purpose we are defining our vision for ourselves in the area we have chosen to work on. And as a result, who we are, who we would like to be and how we want to manifest ourselves in this world.

Here are some thoughts to guide you when you write your vision statement:

As you look back throughout your life there will be a common thread - a desire that has been dominant in your thoughts and actions. You will begin to be able to see projects, movies, books, people and mentors that you automatically gravitated towards or who have gravitated towards you and captured your interest. You also have your own unique gifts, talents, interest, strengths and qualities that are in line with your dreams and visions.

Your vision could be a desire that reigned through your entire life, in situations where you saw other people in action and instantly felt drawn to what they were doing.

Growing up you will find that you have made certain silent statements to yourself that were actually a vision for your life: Such as "When I grow up I want to be an accountant." Or "I would like to be a perfect parent to my kids." Or "I would like to be a world class traveler."

Sometimes you may have a deep conviction and a heart felt desire and passion for a particular cause in the world, that you may want to champion such as "Building a multimillion dollar corporation"; "Feeding starving kids"; "Providing the best education for your kids"; "Contributing to world peace"; "Discovering a solution to a problem in your village town"; "Helping to change your family tree for better"; and so on.

You will also discover that you have qualities, strengths and skills that are in line with the vision you expressed by these statements.

Consider any contributions you would like to make, and the ways you would like to make a difference. In an ideal situation, how best would you be able to contribute to the world, to your family, to your employer or future employer, to your community, to your key relationships? What cause – or causes - would you most like to support?

Here are some useful questions you can ask yourself.

- If I never had to work another day in my life, how would I spend my time?

- At the end of my life, when I look back, what would I regret not doing or achieving?

- As I search my true desires, I might find that there is one desire that has been with me though my entire life. What is that desire?

- If I had one year to live how would I spend that time?

- What one thing would I dare to dream or do, if I knew I could not fail?

- If I could contribute to making a difference in any area of my life or in this world – which area would it be and what difference would I like to make?

- If I inherited or suddenly won a few million dollars, what would I spend my time doing?

- Who am I naturally drawn to? (Which public figure, entrepreneur, professional, artist or person, whether dead or alive?)

- What profession have I always dreamed about?

- What current affair or charity fascinates me?

- Who are my heroes?

- Who inspires me?

- What qualities do I admire most in people?

It is also a great idea to find out what others like about you, not superficially, but the depth of who you are.

You could have had a vision of yourself in various key areas of your life, such as business, family, relationships, career or maybe just a perfect version of the type of person you would like to become, such as the perfect parent, manager, business owner, philanthropist, housewife, employee, corporate citizen, farmer, business tycoon or inventor – whatever area you are drawn to.

Your Vision Statement

When you have gotten in touch with who you are: uncovered your life purpose and clarified your vision this is the "life path" that you need to follow in order to truly be fulfilled as a person. I know that this may sound simpler than it really is, and just knowing your life purpose and having a vision for yourself does not necessarily ensure that you will achieve it.

There are many obstacles and trials we may face along the way. It's as though we are always tested as we move on in life in order to reach to the next levels of development as an evolving soul. We therefore need to develop and incorporate strategies along the way to keep ourselves on target and to spur us on and motivate us. Throughout this book I have provided several strategies and techniques that will enable you to do that. But one I would like to discuss now is developing your vision statement.

What can act as a guiding force in your life and a powerful statement of intention is crafting and documenting your personal vision statement.

A vision statement defines your vision of the desired future outcome you are aspiring to achieve for your life. It should be inspirational and positive. This statement must energize and motivate you towards its attainment and should be written as a power phrase consisting of a few short lines that communicates the essence of your personal values and the purpose of your life.

Here are some examples of my vision statements:

- "A world of empowered people."

- "A world filled with prosperity."

- "A world with perfect health and well being."

- "My loving family that lives in perfect health harmony and prosperity."

- "My perfect being"

- "The realization of all my blessings."

- "A world where every creed and race appreciates the best in each other and lives in peace and harmony."

For some of you with inherent guiding principles and already crafted vision statement - your vision could now be having a better performance than before. You can then use this improved performance as a benchmark for excelling even further.

Now that you have given thought to all of the above you are now ready to craft a personal vision statement for yourself.

Write a short, powerful and impacting statement that conveys the perfect outcome of your vision.

CHAPTER 8

*"There are many things in life that will catch your eye,
but only a few will catch your heart... pursue those."*
Author Unknown

WHAT DO YOU WANT?

Our Dreams And Desires

Many people dream of success and of a life filled with all they desire, but very few realize their dreams because they never do anything strategic to make them a reality. Yet on the other hand there are so many people who think they know what they want, but spend their lives in a state of confusion because they have not taken the time to identify and clarify their dreams, visions, and goals.

Our goals are built on our desires – the things we want in life – and the stronger the desire, the more energy we put into achieving it. Yet a desire on its own is not a goal or dream. A desire maybe fleeting or momentary, and could last a few minutes, a few hours, weeks or months. If it is attached to a core life dream it would last until you have brought that dream to fruition.

Just as desires, our dreams may occupy our thoughts for a moment or may stay with us for months or years or even a lifetime. Each dream creates an image of the future that you will find motivating, and this continues to foster desire.

When you decide what it is you really want out of life (your core dreams and desires)- you will find a way to get it. The human brain has incredible power and can be both the key that will unlock the door to acquiring your heart's desires and the driving force to get what you want.

We all have dreams of what we would like our life to be like and what we would like for ourselves but may have never really taken the time to focus on them.

Now that you've been able to uncover who you really are, and have a vision for your life, it is a good time to take control and clearly decide what it is you want for your life. Deciding what you want is the starting point in developing your pathway to success.

We all deserve to have the very best in life and all of our dreams are important. Why? Because they are our dreams that have been germinating inside of us for a reason. It is our divine right to enjoy the best of what this world has to offer – this is our home and our home is our castle.

The most enriching thing you can do is to take some time for yourself to really listen to your heart and see what dreams would unveil and are ready to be brought to fruition.

Your dreams and desires are not subject to anothers' approval. They are yours and yours alone. Unless your dream is to hurt someone or has negative consequences then have free rein in the dream building-process and allow yourself to dream big. When dreams are nurtured and constantly energized it's easy to convert them into achievable goals, and incorporate them into a workable plan to bring them into your reality. The first step however, is to clearly decide what it is you want and begin to formulate your written list.

As you write, magical things will begin to happen; your focus will act as a laser in identifying all the obstacles and opportunities that are in your path. You become co-creator of your reality beginning with the act of creating your list of desires and dreams. Your clarity will begin to activate them in your life and send out clear messages to the universe that you are ready to achieve your desired outcome.

When you are clear on all that you would like, your clarity will assist you in becoming more focused on getting what you want. You will be pursuing success based on what *you want* and not on someone else's expectation of what success should be for you! When you have listed all that you want, it is an easy task to convert them into achievable goals.

So let's begin this process of identifying your wants

Step 1: Make A List Of Everything You Want

Get in touch with your inner truth and your unique dreams, desires and goals. Look back at the different stages in your life and remember all the dreams you have had for yourself. What are they? Give some deep thought to what you would like to create in your life.

Grab a book or a piece of paper and begin brainstorming, writing everything down until you have exhausted all your ideas. Play some music that you love – get into a happy state of mind as you write your list. Become a little kid again, when we were kids there were no limits to our dreams and everything we did was fun.

Consider each of the various areas of your life using the "Life Analysis List" below, and focus on what you want and are aspiring towards in the various areas of your life.

This "Life Analysis List" is not an exhaustive one, so feel free to add any other categories you would like to work on as you develop your list of goals in those areas. I have also provided some brainstorming questions to use when going through your list.

Jot down everything that comes to mind. Write down every single thing you can think of that you would do and be, if you were perfectly happy and truly fulfilled. Keep on writing and leave nothing out. Nothing is too big or too small to provide the happiness that you are looking for.

Go through the following "Life Analysis List" and understand each category ask yourself:

"What is my idea of the perfect life?"

"What is my idea of the perfect body?"

In doing this exercise, be very explicit and detailed, listing down everything that you want in your life, body, health, relationship and so on.

Life Analysis List:

Personal

- Life
- Health/Body

- Your Family Life/Marriage
- Life-Nurturing and Personal Growth
- Love Life/Romance

Professional

- Career
- Business

Social/Community

- Friends
- Charities
- Social
- World Contribution

Spiritual/Religious

- Groups
- Associations

Financial

- Wealth
- Retirement
- Lifestyle

Family/Children

- Spouse
- Children

- Parents
- Siblings

As you are going through your list – begin by writing and filling out the blanks for the following statement, "I want ....)

Here are some brainstorming questions when going through your list.

- Who would I like to become?
- What would I like to do?
- What would I like to have?
- What would I like to give?
- What do I want to be 1 year from now, 5 years from now, 10 years from now?
- What do I want to earn?
- What do I want to own?
- What do I want to enjoy?
- What activities do I want to participate in?
- What kind of friends and people do I want in my life?
- What dreams and desires have I been carrying inside of me over the past few years?

Do Not Place Limits On Your Dreams

We should be realistic in our planning, but also dream big and never place limits on what it is we can accomplish. In creating your list - do not base your wants and aspirations on your past experiences, in fact, I would urge you to forget your past or current situation in life and list everything that you desire.

Do not place limitations on your dreams or your future. The world is filled with success stories of people who had severe limitations but were able to overcome those challenges and accomplish great things. You can go into any bookstore and walk into the motivation and self-help section and read some of those beautifully written autobiographies.

Never limit you; but allow yourself the opportunity to accomplish your dreams no matter how grand or small they may be. During this process you should also take time to acknowledge all your growth as you face challenges and learn and become a stronger and wiser person. There are stories all around us of people who have made it through every adversity, and kept their dreams in front of them and made them a reality.

Once you know what you really want and it is connected to your life purpose – you and your universal support team will find a way to get it.

Step 2. Separate Your List Into Wants And Goals

Now that you have allowed yourself to list everything that you want, you can separate them into two categories:

- Your want list

- Your goals list.

A. Your Want List

In my opinion, your want list is simply a list of things you would like to do that can be accomplished in a day, a few days or a few weeks. There is very little strategizing involved, as in most instances it's simply a matter of time and money that enables a person to fulfill this list. Some people refer to this want list as your "bucket list". I would also call this your "prize list" or your "rewards to myself list". It can include such things as events you would like to attend, activities to engage in, and things that you would like to buy. Such as:

- wine tasting events

- attending famous plays and other social events

- going to famous restaurants

- places to visit
- seeing your favorite motivational speakers
- going to a particular spa
- buying your favorite top of the line electronics device
- learning to scuba dive
- vacation places you would like to visit and so on

Working on this list is easy and fun and will be a positive spin-off as you accomplish your goals and start to achieve the success that you are looking for.

B. Your Goals List

Having a written list does not mean that you have written down your goals. At this point you have simply listed all your dreams, wants and desires.

In contrast, your goals list can be a bit more complex to attain and can take months and in some instances years to achieve. These form a longer term vision for your life and aspirations. Your goals require much more skills, strategies, planning time and resources for their acquisition.

In order to achieve those dreams and fulfill those desires we need to convert our wants and dreams into achievable goals and in a more tangible state. The goals you put in place will help you to realize them by clearly defining what each one is; and by focusing our attention on each step of the journey towards its achievement and by setting a time frame for it.

Now that you taken out "your want list items" the remaining items can be developed into achievable goals. Here are some examples of goals:

- Establishing a business
- Meeting a financial target for your company
- Getting qualified for a professional career as a lawyer, doctor, accountant and so on

- Transitioning from one career to another
- Meeting a sales target or increasing your existing one
- Planning an exotic family vacation for an average income earner
- Becoming a professional athlete
- Buying a home or investment property
- Starting a charitable foundation

Using your list of wants you have created above, place all the remaining items of your want list on a separate page so that you could begin to start working on a more detailed list of goals.

Some of your goals may not require a detailed action plan – only some very basic planning backed by taking action, while others may require more intricate plans, techniques, strategies, and time to bring into fruition.

In the next few chapters I will go into greater details on everything you need to know about goals since they are such an integral part of living a happy and fulfilled life. We will be covering how to structure and write your goals, examples of effective goal achievement strategies and other essential information that is needed so that you can begin to activate them in your life and be able to send out clear messages to the universe that you are ready to bring them into fruition.

CHAPTER 9

What separates the successful from the unsuccessful is that successful people learn to honor themselves and live their lives being true to their own individuality, while acknowledging the impact of their actions on the people around them and the world at large.
Loana Morgan

CONVERT YOUR WANTS INTO ATTAINABLE GOALS

Goal-Setting - Making Your Dreams A Reality…

What is a goal? In its simplest form, it is the end result of what you want to achieve. Goals give us the ability to create our future in advance and can stimulate the power that will enable us to grow, expand, and navigate our pathway to success.

Successful business people and achievers in all fields use key techniques and strategies to set their goals. These techniques and strategies assist them in deciding exactly what they want to accomplish and how they can systematically chart their course to get there.

Setting goals is a powerful way to boost your performance and when approached properly, your efforts translate into commitment and ultimately into results. People with clear goals succeed because they know exactly where they are going. And they have rehearsed both mentally and on paper how they are going to get there are able to identify and prepare for any potential problems that may be encountered along the way.

Here are a few of the benefits of goal-setting:

- We dream of the future and live in the present and goals provide us with short-term and long-term visions for our lives. The more powerful our goals, the greater our probability of overcoming obstacles and achieving success along the way. It is our long-term vision of the outcome that helps us to get past any short-term obstacles.

- Our goals, when properly planned and carefully navigated, can produce our reality. As you document your dreams and desires, and convert them into achievable goals you summon what you want from the non-physical realm and bring it into the physical realm, giving life to it. In doing so, you are able to plan your life rather than merely take it as it comes.

- You become successful the moment you start moving towards your goals or begin walking in the direction of your dreams. Your dreams, desires, and goals are like a compass that guides you through your journey of life. People with clear goals succeed because they know exactly where they are going.

- When clarified and properly documented you will be able to clearly decipher what you want and how best to achieve them in all areas of your life.

- When you work towards a challenging goal, you feel motivated and inspired, with a sense of direction and purpose in life.

- One of the great benefits of setting a goal is the person you will become in the process of accomplishing it. In the pursuit of your goals you will always become more. Goals cause us to stretch and grow in ways that we have never done before, because in order to reach our goals we must adjust and grow. In the process we end up becoming a person of far greater value to ourselves and those around us and as an extension – the world at large.

In order to get you more aligned to having success with the goals you are aspiring to achieve, the following section on goal-setting covers beginner, intermediate techniques and some more advanced methods that are easy to implement on your own.

When you are beginning to work on your goals please ensure that you are comfortable with the one you have chosen to start working on. If you are not, then begin by working on smaller goals that are easier to accomplish. This would get you into the habit and create the discipline needed for setting goals and achieving them. Once you are able to accomplish a few of the smaller goals it will then become a lot easier to succeed at achieving longer-term or larger goals. The choice is ultimately yours to make.

A Note For Advance Goal Setters:

There is more advanced information that I could discuss. However, I believe that unless you have practiced some form of goal-setting for a number of years, the more advanced techniques could overwhelm you. Sometimes less is more and in order to master the more advanced techniques, we must first become masters of the foundation - and get the process started.

I have found that if someone has been practicing goal setting techniques or is following a plan to achieve goals but not getting the desired results, there could be some core reasons that are unique to that person's past experiences in life or in business. These reasons will need to be dealt with on a more professional level in order to uncover the root cause that may be preventing the success they are looking for. There may be a need for more advanced techniques that require one-to-one or small focus group interactive coaching.

Essential Strategies In Writing Goals To Get The Results You Want

The way that you write your goals is very important. A well-written goal could contribute to at least 30% of the manifesting process, if the goal setter has reached the level necessary to take it to the next level.

There is an old saying "be careful what you wish for, because you will surely get it." This is especially applicable with your goals. In order to begin the process of achieving your goals you need to be able to clearly define them as opposed to leaving them vague and ambiguous. You must be specific and clear, since your Higher Self and the Higher Power and the universe need clear direction before they can begin to manifest exactly what it is you would like.

Since the achievement of your goals make the difference in your quality of life; fulfilling your life purpose and the person you become; it is important that you spend time working on it.

Here are some useful tips and guidelines on how to convert your remaining items on your want list into achievable goals:

Assume A Posture Of Confidence

- Set your goals from a place of knowing and expectancy and assume a posture of confidence as you write down your goals. Be in a peak state of possibilities.

Specify Well Crafted Outcome

- In writing your goals it is very important to have well-crafted outcomes since successful goal achievers have large, detailed, clear mental pictures and clearly stated goals with a defined outcome of what they want to achieve.

Be Clear About The Conditions

- It is not just important to specify what it is you want, you must also be clear about the conditions surrounding it, especially with goals that are going to consume most of your efforts and energy, such as your lifelong goals. (It is my belief that if those goals are in line with your destiny, life has a way of working things out for its attainment. But there are boundaries that you need to set for yourself in order to be safe and have the best that life has to offer).

Be Very Specific And Detailed

- Be very specific and detailed as to what it is you would like to accomplish. The more details your write about your goals, the clearer your outcome. For example don't say "I'd like to make more money in this upcoming New Year." Be very specific and state exactly how much money you would like to earn. Each goal should be positively stated and as specific as possible.

Set Realistic Timelines and Milestones

- Your goals should be written with realistic timelines and milestones and be measurable so that you can track your progress to see whether you are on course with the deadlines you have set for yourself.

Use Positive Simple Language

- Goals should be written in positive and simple inspiring language. They should motivate and inspire you into action! When your goals are positively written you will attract the positive results you are looking for.

Your Goals Should Complement And Support Each Other

- Your goals should complement and support each other and not be contradictory in way. You cannot have a goal to have a balanced life with your family and be there for the kids and at the same time aspire to a career or business that takes you away from them most of the time. This would result in an internal conflict that creates a great deal of guilt and stress. Your goals must be supportive of each other and mutually reinforcing. (There may be times when sacrifices will have to be made but always maintain your vision right in front of you and re-focus in order to get back on track.)

Develop Long Range Goals

- Be sure to set big goals as this will force you to reach deep within and use the potential that is inside you. Long-range goals help you to overcome short-range failures. They can also help you to change your direction without going back on your decision.

Examples of Converting Your Wants Into Achievable Goals

Here are two examples on how you would convert your list into achievable goals to begin manifesting them and bringing it from a desired state to the physical realm. I have decided to use two important areas of our lives that most people can relate to.

Example 1: Goal - To Obtain Your Dream Job

This is such as important area of our life. We spend most of our waking hours in our career and business and should aspire for the one that we love and enjoy. In honoring ourselves and what we truly want, we are able to make a positive and healthy contribution to ourselves, our family and the company we work for. Why spend your life in a career that saps your energy or with people who have no respect for what you are worth?

You do have lots of choices, simply look at any job boards on the websites or in newspapers and you will see the multitude of jobs available!

Here are the steps in converting your wants into achievable, manifesting goals:

The very first thing is to focus on all that you would like in your ideal job. Here are a few questions to assist you:

- What is the ideal job that you have always dreamed about or would like to have?

- Are you looking for full-time or part-time work? If part-time, how many hours?

- What kind of people would you like to work for?

- What kind of leaders and management would you like to work with?

- What sort of work environment would you like? (casual, corporate or a combination)

- What are the best companies that offer the type of jobs you are looking for?

- What salary range are you expecting?

- Which geographical area are you willing to work in?

- What type of industry would you be happy in that suits your skills, abilities and desires.

- By when would you like to get your new job?

- Clearly decide what is negotiable or non-negotiable for your job expectations.

Make your list as detailed, specific and as clear as possible.

Here is an example of how you might write your goal:

"My goal is to get a management job in my field, earning $10,000 per month with full car allowance and benefits. I would like to work an 8- hour job during the hours of 9 to 5 within a 20 km radius from my home in a large corporation that has room for professional growth. In this job I will be working with people I can learn from and whom I respect and admire and who respect and admire me. There is great teamwork!"

Example 2: Goal – To Find The Perfect Relationship

Most people are in search of meaningful, positive and loving relationships in their life. If we examine our close relationships, we may discover that they are a reflection of our own feelings of self-worth. Positive people surround themselves with others who treat them with respect, recognize and value them for who they are and operate in a relationship of truth, love, support and integrity.

You need to decide what it is you are looking for in a person and relationship before you start looking for the perfect person. Here are a few questions to assist you.

- Clearly decide the type of person you are looking for and
- The type of relationship you want.
  - Are you looking for a short-term or long-term relationship?
  - Are you looking for a casual relationship with no commitment or more meaningful ones?
- Who is your ideal guy or girl?
  - How do they look physically?
  - How are they mentally, emotionally and spiritually?
  - What qualities you would like in that person?
  - What personality and traits would you like them to have? (Do you want someone with an adventurous spirit, serious or calm and steady or a combination of all?)

- What professional and personal development are you looking for in that person?

- What values and beliefs would you like that person to have?

- What common personality traits would you like them to share?

- What cultural or religious backgrounds are you looking for?

Clearly decide what is negotiable and non-negotiable in your expectations of the person you are looking for. What habits and traits are you not willing to put up with or compromise on? It is always a good practice to set your boundaries early in a relationship.

Articulating Powerful Intentions For Goals Attainment.

In addition to effectively writing your goals, another important area that we have to consider is the way we articulate powerful intentions for goal attainment.

Articulating powerful intentions is like a powerful magnet that draws what it is you want to accomplish. It is very important that you are explicit with the way you set your intentions before and during the process of visualizing, talking, thinking and writing down your goals. Your intentions energetically begin the process of attracting and drawing to you all that you are aspiring towards achieving.

As much as you can engage all your senses to attract the outcome you are hoping to achieve. A simple way to do this is by writing, saying, feeling and imagining your desire as if it were real and you were already in possession of it.

There are two powerful ways that I would like to suggest for articulating your intentions when setting personal and business goals. They are:

Business Goals

Your business goals are something that you would like in the future. Its outcome is dependent on some present or future action that you need to take in order to have the results that you are looking for. Therefore, when you are working on setting any business goals they should be stated (either verbally or written) in the following way:-

"**As I commence** my job search *I am attracting* my ideal job that provides everything I want, such as (list all the qualities that you are looking for in a perfect career).

This is such a powerful concept that provides greater clarity and results. I have seen many people use a present-tense statement for a future goal and incorporated it into their affirmations and plans thereby energizing it. In doing so, they were able to draw it to themselves quickly but were not ready to handle the success that came and as a result they ended up failing in maintaining the outcome.

Sometimes they may not be ready as a person for that level, since with every level of development comes greater responsibilities and skills that are needed. We must be ready and prepared for the success we are aspiring to achieve. Success is a journey that provides the experience that is needed for all that we are aspiring towards.

When you would like to attract something in your life say – "I am attracting prosperity in all that I do." "I am attracting happiness." There is something powerfully surreal that happens when you speak this way, it's as though everything is already there for you, you simply have to take action and be in a total state of expecting to receive.

Personal Change Goals

Your Personal Change Goals are something you would like to have happen immediately. It is an instant change in you would like to achieve and are ready to do so *now*, not sometime in the future.

When you are setting your Personal Change Goals it should be stated in the present tense, as follows:

To become Confident say:

- I, Jane Smith am confident

To have Perfect Health say:

- I, Jane Smith am in perfect health

Other misc statements you can say

- I, Jane Smith am happy

- I, Jane Smith am action oriented and dynamic

- I, Jane Smith am protected at every level in every part of me

When you write in the present tense you are telling the universe that's the way it should be and you are also affirming the way you want it to be here and now. Not sometime in the future but *now*. In doing so you are giving it more power to manifest soon.

Speak of your outcome in your life as though you have already attained it. Do not say "I want" or "I would like" or "I wish." Instead say "I am" or "I have." For example when you are seeking good health say, "I am healthy," "I am successful," "I am happy."

A statement becomes even more powerful when you add your name in front of it. As an example you could say "I Jane Smith am attracting my perfect life partner, with these qualities (and state the qualities that you would like in that person)."

In order to be in alignment with the person you are meant to be you need to change your awareness from what you don't want to what you do want. Then stay in that state, in order to become the kind of person to draw to yourself all that is needed.

CHAPTER 10

*Some people worry that if they do what is right
for themselves they will be acting in a selfish way
when you honor your higher path and self,
you always honor the higher path and self of
others, even if it does not seen so at the time.*
Sanaya Roman

IS THIS WHAT YOU REALLY WANT?

It is so important to consider the life you would be living in your new role once you have achieved your goals. Consider all angles and how it might affect all aspects of your life; don't just look at the positive outcomes; but consider the negative outcomes as well. You especially need to do this with goals that will demand a lot from you and will take a long period of your time and resources to attain.

Sometimes the achievement of your goals and having success in some areas of your life, may produce problems in other areas. It is therefore a good idea to stop and evaluate your most important goals that you are aspiring towards and:

1. Conduct a reality check

2. Evaluate whether your goals align to your vision

3. Wear your goal to see if they fit

4. Check the ecology of your goals

I know that many of you may be asking, "Why should I do this after I have spent so much time doing all the above work in the previous chapters?"

Conducting this reality check enables you to evaluate the larger impact it would have on all areas of your life and on your circle of influence especially your loved ones. Very often I have seen people get caught up in euphoria and developed their goals and plans based on the situation they are in or the group of people that influenced them or the relationship they were involved in that had a major influence in their life.

During that time their thought patterns were highly influenced by that association and a tremendous amount of their decision-making evolved from it. Only to realize years later when they left that sphere of influence that the things they thought they wanted were based on someone else's dreams and not their own or did not fulfill the need they were aiming for. During that time they may have invested a tremendous amount of time, money and effort into something that was not part of their greater destiny!

To clearly decide:

- if the goals you are pursuing are what you really want, and
- how it would affect the other areas of your life and the people being impacted, and
- if you are willing to commit to what it takes to achieve them, you should do the following:

1. Conduct A Reality Check

Before you start working on your plan for achieving your goals you should take a few minutes and look at each of your goals and ask yourself *"**Is this what I would truly like to accomplish?**"*

When conducting your reality check it is a good idea to fast forward to having attained them and evaluate the effects they would have in key areas of your life once you have attained your outcome. Ask yourself these questions regarding your top goals:

What are the implications of achieving my goals?

- What will I gain if I achieve these goals?
- How would I gain financially?

- What positive impact would it have in my life?

- How would having accomplished those goals make me feel emotionally and mentally?

- What positive impact would it have in my spiritual, professional, personal, social life or my overall well being?

- What would I no longer have to tolerate that I dislike in my life?

- What will it mean for my family if I obtain this outcome?

- How would it change my life for the better?

- What are some of the pleasures I would have in achieving these goals?

- How would it change my life for the worse?

What are the implications of not achieving my goals?

- What would I lose by not achieving my goals?

- What might be the benefits of not achieving my goals?

- What would not achieving this goal cost me financially, emotionally, and mentally?

- How would this failure reflect on me as a person? How would I view myself?

- How would my family view me?

- How would society view me?

Am I willing to commit to these goals?

- Does it have sufficient importance for me to be fully committed to achieving it?

- Do I really want these goals?

- Will the results be worth the time, resources and effort involved?

- What will it mean for me when I attain my goals?

- Will attaining these goals demand more from me?

- What will it cost me personally and for how long?

- Am I a family person? Will it take me away from the people I love?

- Am I willing to pay that price?

- Can I truly commit to fulfilling all that it will require?

2. Do Your Goals Align With Your Vision?

Now that you have listed all your goals it is a good idea to decide if they are consistent with your vision, and whether they have sufficient importance for you to fully commit to achieving them?

When your goals are in alignment with your core life purpose then accomplishing those goals and dreams will add to the fulfillment of your soul purpose here on earth.

One of the ways to decide this, is to determine what higher purpose they will serve in your life and in what way does achieving them align with the vision for your life.

Fast forward to having attained them and see the effects it would have with the vision of your future.

Conduct a review of your goals and ask yourself if they are consistent with the vision you have of yourself and do they truly represent an extension of who you are when you have attained them. Do they get you closer to realizing your vision or are they totally unrelated to it?

- Are they fulfilling in all aspects of your life?

- Does achieving your goals bring you closer to or take you further away from that vision?

- Does it add value to, or compliment your vision?

When your goals are in line with your vision you are naturally motivated and driven to achieve them and there is also a greater level of commitment on your part.

3. **Wear Your Outcome And See If It Fits**

How many of you know someone who has worked very hard to accomplish their goals, only to realize it's not what they want or what they expected it to be? To prevent this from happening to you, try walking the outcome in your mind's eye and go through the following:

- Can I see myself clearly in this new role?

- What does it take to commit to this role?

- What are the wider implications?

- Who else would be impacted as I live this outcome?

- Does the achievement of this goal mean that I have just started this new journey and it is not the end all, but the beginning of another one?

- Do I need to fulfil any expectations?

- Do I have what it takes to fulfil those expectations?

- Am I 100% committed in that role?

- Can I commit to and fulfil the obligations that come with having achieved the successful outcome of my goal?

- Now that I have achieved it what else is expected of me?

- Does it fit into who I am and my major beliefs and values?

- Is it what I really want?

Look at other people who are in the role that you want.

- How are they?

- Are they truly happy?

4. Check The Ecology Of Your Goals

Your goals should be ecological and never cause hurt to anyone. We do not live independently of each other and need to live in the awareness that the attainment of our goals would have an impact on the people around us.

I have seen companies or people who went after success and did not care whom they hurt or destroyed in the process. In order to gain financial success or for power and control they used "whatever means possible" to acquire their goals while invading people's lives and infringing on their rights as human beings.

I have also seen people chase after power and position for all the wrong reasons and ended up totally unfulfilled, or having a devastating effects on those who looked up to them for leadership and guidance and in some instances protection. Some of them spent their entire lives chasing after something that is not meant to be theirs in the first place, wrongfully believing that it could have filled a gap in their life. This is usually the behavior of someone who never really took the time to understand his or her role in the overall scheme of things.

I know that there are times when short-term sacrifices have to be made, but it does not mean that those have to turn into long-term ones. It is important to always strive for balance in all that you do.

There were people who went doggedly after their goals without ever considering the repercussions on their spouse, their loved one and/or their family members. They actually operated with a belief that if they achieved success their family would benefit no matter what the cost of repercussions. Yet, they never stopped to ask their loved ones if that is what they wanted. In the process, they ended up losing the very thing that was their drive and motivation for success in the first place.

No matter what the rewards, I believe that we must always live by the "Golden Rule" – "do unto others as you would have them do unto you". That rule has proven to be a great measuring rod for us to see if the actions we are taking are beneficial to all concerned including ourselves.

Before plunging ahead it is important in your goal achievement process that you consider the people whose lives will be impacted as you would want the same for yourself.

People are so precious and need to be treated with respect, care and compassion and a high level of integrity. Make it a habit to always ask yourself:

> "How will pursuing and achieving my goal affect my loved ones and society? Will it have a negative or positive impact on them"?

Honor yourself and those around you and always check the ecology of your goals, be true to yourself and those around you and the outcome and impact of your action will have far reaching positive impact even after you have left this earth.

CHAPTER 11

*You were really born to win
However in order to be the winner,
that you were born to be
you have got to plan to win…
you have got to prepare to win…
And then you expect and accept your win!
Zig Ziglar*

THE POWER OF A PLAN

Dreams, visions and goals can only take you so far. In order bring them into a reality, they must to be supported by a real plan with effective strategies and the proper follow-up actions.

Your dreams create images of a future that you find motivating and this builds the desire. The dream is what you want and the desire is how you feel about wanting it. By developing a plan, you are able to realize your dreams and can focus your attention on each step of the journey.

Developing a clear specific blueprint for achieving your goals is critical for your success. Every major corporation utilizes this powerful visioning and planning technique, yet so few of us apply it to what should be our most important focus – our life.

The majority of people spend more time planning their vacations than they do planning for success, happiness, and the various achievements they desire in life. Would you head off on a journey to a new territory without a map? Of course not; yet if you are like most people, you are living your life without a map or a clear plan of where you would like to go.

A properly developed plan provides the competitive edge among people with similar resources who are striving towards achieving the same goal. It determines the few who actually achieves their goals and those who will excel way beyond others.

In order to win at the game of life we need to prepare ourselves fully with the best techniques and tools that are available. We need to become a master navigator on our way to manifesting our dreams, goals, and objectives in order to succeed.

Writing down your goals adds energy and clears your pathway to success and will definitely increase your odds of succeeding! The clearer you are about your goals and what you need to do in order to achieve them, the easier it will be for you to succeed!

Here are a few of the benefits to be derived from developing your goal-achievement plan:

It Gives You The Competitive Edge

Planning is such an important part of succeeding in all that you do. A plan prepares you to be fully resourced - mentally, emotionally and physically in the achievement of your goals and will enable you to sustain your growth and take you to higher levels; it gives you the competitive edge. (Should you so desire)

You Can Pro-actively Create Your Life

Your plan enables you to become an active participant in creating your life, with great measure of control over your destiny. You are able to proactively take charge rather than react to whatever life throws at you!

You Can Gain Clarity In Your Thinking

As you develop your plans, you will gain clarity in your thinking and be able to pinpoint precisely what you would need in order to achieve your goals. In gaining clarity you are able to devise effective goal-acquisition strategies to properly navigate your path and be able to harness your inner resources while learning and growing.

You Can Mentally Rehearse The Various Steps Of Your Plan

By documenting your goals and the steps you need to accomplish them, you will be able to mentally rehearse walking the path to success. You will be able to visualize and fine-tune your plan while adding strategies or making improvements every step of the way.

You Can Be Able To Track Your Progress

This is your plan of action to stay on course and be able to achieve your goals faster. As you continue to work on your plan, you can track your progress towards meeting targets and goals and anticipate how long it will take to reach your destination.

You will be also able to see what is working and what isn't and modify your plan to get yourself on track for your achievement.

Low Value Activities Will Be Eliminated

When properly done, you can eliminate all unnecessary activities and low value tasks resulting in saving time and money. You will maximize your time effectively in reaching your goals.

You Can Anticipate Obstacles And Problems

A properly prepared and "well thought through" plan will be able to predict in advance most of the obstacles you may encounter. This will assist you to make any necessary adjustments to your overall strategies and overcome obstacles and setbacks. As a "spin off" benefit you can learn from mistakes and change limitations into opportunities.

You Can Develop Focus

You develop the focus that you need to attain your goals faster and more easily and as a result, become mentally and emotionally prepared to tackle any situation that could potentially arise.

You Can Hold Yourself Accountable

You set deadlines and established milestones for your plans. You can categorize your goals into short-term and intermediate objectives so you can measure your progress and be alerted if you are getting off course. You can hold yourself accountable to the deadlines you have set or you can get a trusted partner or coach to guide you along the way.

You Can Gain Knowledge And Experience And Grow

You simply cannot help but grow as you set out to accomplish your goals. There are many times you may be challenged or may have to push yourself to the limit. The knowledge and growth that results from stretching to reach your goals are rewarding in themselves.

You Can Craft Better, More Effective Strategies

When developing your plans, you can work on each step and each process along the way. When seemingly impossible goals are being tackled, effective strategies can be crafted so that you are better prepared to handle them in bite size chunks making them easier to achieve.

Eliminate Costly Mistakes

Talk to any successful person you know and you will realize how hard they work at their goals and the numerous sacrifices and costly mistakes in time and money they made along the way. Incorporating this powerful "goal achievement" tool gives you the strategic edge in transforming your life and making your dreams a reality. It gives you the ability to eliminate costly mistakes and wasted time and to focus completely on results oriented activities.

Be Prepared To Make Sacrifices

Success is a choice that we make, supported by a well thought through plan and key strategies backed by hard work, determination, drive, and flexibility!

What this journey makes of you will always be of equal if not far greater value than your specific accomplishments.

Be prepared to make sacrifices to achieve your goals in order to walk in your greatness by manifesting all that your life was destined to be. We each have our destiny and have been ordained for what we are to become; that destiny is our God-given right to achieve.

To aid and simplify this process, I have developed and included a goal-setting workbook. Go on to my Website www.loanamorgan.com and register indicating that you have purchased a copy of the book and I will send you a free copy of it. When you have read through all the goal setting chapters and are ready to develop your plan, all you need to do is to print and work through the workbook. This is such a valuable tool.

There are many goal-achievement plans out there but the one I describe in the next section is very close to my heart. I know that implementing this plan or some elements of it would give you greater leverage in creating the life that you were meant to live and would enable far greater control over your future.

So let's get right into it and begin to develop your plan of action and implement key strategies so that you can produce results that surpass past performance and *design a life perfectly tailored for you.*

CHAPTER 12

When you follow your bliss…
doors will open where you would
not have thought there would be doors;
and where there wouldn't
be a door for anyone else.
Joseph Campbell

DEVELOPING YOUR PLAN FOR SUCCESS

We are all searching for the magic formula and the perfect plan, but each of us is unique and motivated differently. We need to develop the magic formula and plan that works for us and fits our style and personality. As we follow our plan we can add our personality to it, so that we can get the results that are perfect to our expectations and circumstances.

You have written your vision statement; you're clear about what you want and have set your goals. Are you committed to transforming them into a reality? Let's take control of your life and your destiny and allow yourself to plan and rehearse your journey in advance. It is now time to develop your detailed plans and describe how you intend to go about achieving them.

Developing Your Plan Of Success

There is no cookie cutter approach or "the perfect plan" that will work for everyone. As unique individuals with our own preferred style of doing things, what might motivate one person may not necessarily motivate another. Some people love to plan everything down to the minutest detail and then monitor each action on a daily basis. They love to work through all the intricate details and ensure that everything is done in an orderly manner.

On the other hand, there are others who simply prefer to write down their overall goals and let things unfold. These are people who would unconsciously follow their plans and "take charge" without a lot of details and simply deal with challenges as they arise.

My advice to you is to realize that what is important are the results you are getting from your actions. If what you are doing works for you, then great, continue along the same path! Keep on doing it. However, if you are not getting the results you are looking for you should try something else. If necessary, you can always adjust your style in order to gain the results you are looking for – since flexibility is such an important part of succeeding in anything you do.

It is also a good idea to leave your possibilities open to a benevolent universe of a loving and ethical nature to also deliver wonderful surprises throughout your life.

Express yourself in your own unique way and go with whatever style of goal setting you can have the most fun with and implement without it being a bore or a chore. Allow yourself the flexibility of learning, growing and having fun with it. What separates the successful from others is that successful people learn to honor themselves and live their lives while being true to their own individuality, the impact of their actions on the people around them and the world at large.

In developing your plans you are making short-term sacrifices for long-term gain. And what might appear to be a great deal of work in the beginning is actually what will save you time, money, and sweat in the long run and provide the greatest form of happiness and fulfillment long-term.

Be the captain of your new life and chart your own course by designing the blue print of your desired life. As you read the following steps, feel free to "loop back" to any section on this book that adds clarity and value to whatever it is you are working on.

Step 1: Select Your Top 3 to 5 Goals

Now that you are certain about the goals you want to accomplish. Take a few moments and analyze your list and:

- Select the top 3 to 5 most important goals,

- the ones that are going to reap you the greatest rewards and benefits.

- the goals which when achieved, would provide the greatest positive impact either in business or in your life and move you closer towards your happiness and fulfillment.

- the goals and dreams which best support your personal vision statement and are most important to you at this time in your life.

Once you have taken out your top goal:

1. Place a rating (in order of priority) on all the other goals that you plan on pursuing after.

2. Begin to work on your top goal immediately.

By focusing on the most important goals that need to be accomplished, you are able to harness your resources in the most productive and efficient manner. You will build momentum, and through exponential growth will be able to bring massive leverage in manifesting those specific goals. You will eliminate all unnecessary items that waste your time and resources.

Step 2. List All The Action Steps Needed

For each of the goals that you have selected above, ask yourself –

- **"What action steps do I need to take in order to achieve my goals?"**

Once you have started, simply continue to ask yourself.

- **"What is the next action that is needed to get me closer to achieving my goals?"**

A brainstorming session can help you identify what's needed to bridge the gap between your desired goals and its achievement. This very important step will let you know in advance, almost everything you will need to accomplish your goals.

- Brainstorm and make a list of every activity that you need in order to achieve your goals and outline all that are needed in order to execute them.

- You've now listed the various steps needed to start working on your plan.

- Once you have completed it, place it in sequential order of activities.

Step 3. Break Down Your Complex Steps To Achievable Ones

From your activity list above there may be longer term and complex action steps that are needed. In order to accomplish them you may need to break down all your challenging and longer term activities into smaller achievable ones.

This will make them more manageable to handle and allow you better control in achieving success.

Once you have done this, organize them into the right flow that is needed to start taking actions!

Step 4. Set Time Frames And Priorities

Your next task is to take a few minutes to prioritize and set timelines and milestones for each action step before you plunge ahead working on your plan.

By breaking down your goals into action steps and setting applicable milestones, you are establishing standards for measuring your progress.

Decide which goals are going to be:

- Short-term goals

- Mid-term goals

- Long-term goals

Ask yourself:

- What is my deadline for the accomplishment of my goal?

- How much time will it take to achieve or complete my task?

- Do I have the time needed for success? If not, can I reallocate my time and activities in order to free up some time?

- If I do not have the time, do I need to adjust my deadline?

Schedule your steps so that you can track your progress. Set your milestones and deadlines so that you can have a date of achievement to aim towards

- Now that you have established those milestones and deadlines, place them next to each step.

Even though you have set deadlines, be flexible, life happens – bringing with it unexpected changes and challenges, make adjustments to suit. A step back can sometimes mean a few steps forward!

Step 5. What Else Is Needed To Accomplish Your Goals

Now that you have listed all the activities that are needed and have set your timelines and milestones, you will need to work on all that are needed for the fruition of your goals. Ask yourself: "Now that I have listed all the action needed, what will I need to achieve my goals?"

This is a very simple process that allows you to evaluate all that is needed to fulfill all the steps above and meet your desired outcome. For each of the goals you have selected and the actions needed consider which of the following you would need:

Resources:

People

- Is this something I can do by myself or do I need help?

- If I need help, who do I need to help me accomplish my goals?

For business goals you may need to engage the services of professionals who are able to provide the expertise you are in need of, such as service providers, consulting, marketing, advertising and so on.

For personal goals you may need to include your family members such as your spouse or kids.

Internal Resources

Evaluate all the internal resources you will need to fulfill your goals.

- Such as knowledge, confidence, attitude, skill, abilities and energy levels.

Skills and Training

Evaluate the skills and training that are needed in order to prepare you for obtaining your goals and also for being able to fully utilize it, once it has been achieved. Ask yourself:

- What skills do I need to acquire in order to achieve my goals?

- Do I possess those skills? If no, what do I need to do in order to acquire them?

- Do I need to undergo any training in order to prepare myself to achieve my goals? Or to be able to fully utilize the benefits of my goals once I have achieved it?

Financial

Evaluate your financial needs. Ask yourself:

- What financial resources would I need?

- How much money would I need?

- Do I need all of it now and or can it be allocated over a period of time?

- If allocated over a period of time, how much do I need at each phase of the project?

- Do I have the financial resources needed?

- If not, where can I find it?

- Is there an alternative way of accomplishing my goals with less resources and achieving the same results?

Assets/Furniture/Fixtures

Evaluate all the assets/furniture/fixtures needed. Ask yourself:

- What raw materials or assets, office, furniture, electronics and fixtures such as desk, computers, telephones, computer software and so on do I need?

Step 6. Take Action

So you have developed your plan. It is now time to take action and start working on it. Taking action fuels the engine and sets everything in motion in the process of achieving your goals and dreams.

Understand that the only way to achieve your goals is to take action and make it happen! You can take the time to do all the exercises above and take no action and wait for fate to decide, but chances are you won't achieve what you are aiming for.

Every action taken will get you closer and closer to the accomplishment of your goals and develop discipline needed. You will create the momentum needed to propel yourself toward success and as you continue to take action you will begin to see accelerated growth in your area of focus.

Be proactive and take action immediately. Think of one simple thing you can do today which will move you nearer to your goal, and then act on it immediately.

I suggest that you identify all the critical areas and priority items that need to be addressed first and do those tasks immediately.

Focus on all the priority items you have listed and start working towards them even if it is simply grabbing a note book and conceptualizing on paper or engaging in something else you need to work on for your goals.

The value and benefit you receive from taking action will inspire and motivate you to move on to the next action needed and then the next and so on.

Step 7. Review Your Progress And Practice Flexibility

There is a balance to be found between throwing caution to the wind and depending on fate to deliver what it is you are hoping for, and steering your own life course. When what you're doing is working, that's great and when it isn't – it's time to do something else. Don't fight against the current. Exercise wisdom in all that you do and find ways to move along the flow of your life.

Once you have begun to take action it is a good practice to stop periodically and reflect on and evaluate the results you are getting and determine what is working and what is not

As you go along, monitor your actions and be aware of what's happening with the strategies you are implementing and the results you are getting. As needed you can re-strategize and adjust your timelines. This is where it is also important to follow your intuition and pay attention to your inner guidance system.

Ask yourself these questions:

- Am I on schedule in meeting the targets I had hoped to accomplish by now?

- If not, what do I need to do in order to get back on track?

- Which part of my plan is not working out?

- Is there something missing?

- Do I need to re-strategize?

- Do I need help from external sources?

It always a good time to reflect and refocus if needed in order to either stay on course or maybe move on to something else. Revisit and revise your plan regularly, especially when you get new information or when things are not going as you had expected.

If, after giving it your best you are still struggling, pushing and working hard and not achieving the expected results, you may need to consider that you're not being true to yourself or focusing your energy in the most effective way. You may even need to go back and get some professional advice or set new goals, or smaller goals and work your way up to the larger ones.

Always, give yourself the chance to succeed while staying open to other new opportunities around you. Notice what results your actions are producing and develop the flexibility and willingness to change or fine tune your strategies, actions or goals in order to achieve your desired outcome. Use your energy, time and resources wisely.

Strategies

Implementing the right strategies is so very important in the attainment of your goals that I have dedicated the next chapter to it.

HIGHER LEVELS OF ATTAINMENT – MOVING BEYOND GOAL SETTING

This is the beginning of a brand new day and
God has given to me this day to do with it what I please
I can waste the whole day or I can use it for good
But what I choose to do today is extremely important because
I am exchanging a whole day of my life for what I choose to do with my time
So when tomorrow comes leaving in its place
something I have exchanged for it…
I want that to be **good** and not evil
I want it to be **success** and not failure
I want it to be **gain** and not loss
In order that I will never regret the price I paid for this day
Naomi Rhode

CHAPTER 13

*We are made wise not by recollections of our past
but by the responsibility for our future.*
George Bernard Shaw

STRATEGIES FOR SUCCESS

When you are clear on all your goals and plans how you achieve success and accomplish your goals will be evident to you. *You are now pursuing success based on what you would like and not someone else's expectation of what you should be doing.*

Going through the previous chapters should get some of you at least 30 - 40% of the way towards success in achieving your goals. (It may be less or more depending on the level you were at in your growth and development before you started working on your plans). For some people the percentage will be even higher. What will contribute to the differences are the strategies you use along the way and your level of expertise and experience.

Since the readers of this book will have their own individual goals, it is very difficult for me to craft and pinpoint precise strategies that are specific to your unique goals and objectives. The fact is, as you continue to implement your goal-achievement plans, the most effective strategies will begin to unfold as you make progress each step along the way. There are a variety of ways you will obtain the strategies needed. You can find them though research, seminars, books and people who have succeeded in the field of your chosen endeavor. Once you have committed to your goals and it is part of your life purpose, your universal support team will direct and provide you with the answers you need.

Your strategies are your ideas and techniques designed specifically to achieve your unique goals.

As such, I am providing you with a few key overall strategies that are essential to any goal-achievement plan. I have begun with a series of questions that you can ask yourself regarding your specific goals in order to stimulate the right thought processes and help you become more resourceful in coming up with the right strategies. So let's get into it:

Brainstorm strategies needed for your plans through the use of questions. For each goal you have selected ask yourself:

- What are the best people in my field doing that has made them successful?

- What are some of the latest techniques available for me to utilize in pursuing my goals?

- Who can I turn to for advice or guidance?

- What time-management techniques can I implement that will help me to accomplish my goals within the timeframe I have set for it?

- Who do I need to become in order for me to achieve this goal?

- What changes do I need to make in my life to become that person?

- What professional or personal development do I need in order to prepare myself for the role that I am undertaking?

- What unique actions or, tools and techniques can I implement in order to develop the competitive edge in achieving my goals?

Now that you have answered the above and were able to pinpoint some unique strategies for implementation in your plan, here are some strategies you can engage in.

1. Act In Alignment With Your Outcome

A very important strategy you can implement that can push you further along in succeeding with your goals is to begin to consciously and intentionally assist in the creation of the future you desire. If you expect to achieve results in life and business that you have never accomplished before, you will need to become the person that is needed to fulfill that destiny and be able to attract all the success that you expect to achieve.

One of the fastest ways to get into alignment with your outcome and become a vibration match for what you want to draw into your life is to begin to act as if your success is certain and as though you have already attained it. I have seen many people talk right and walk left and sabotage their own success. Live with the belief that what you want is already yours.

You need to immediately start acting as the person you would like to become. I am not talking about living an extravagant lifestyle, your thoughts and actions must be consistent with the person you want to become and the role you would like to assume.

I am referring to your words, your manner, your attitude, your dress, your posture and your actions. They should all be consistent with the ideal you and as though you have already accomplished your goals and dreams. Emulate the mannerisms and qualities of successful people in the area in which you are seeking to gain success.

This alignment of your thought, feelings and actions will attract what you have aligned yourself with as a result of the Laws of Attraction.

You need to live your outcome as though it has already occurred – you have got to focus on the ideal situation. From this moment forward act as if your success is certain. Keep your focus fixed on the outcome. Behave as though your success is guaranteed. During this process when doubts and skepticism come your way, simply observe them and let them go. Act as though you have complete faith and back it up with consistent action and key strategies and move forward with total conviction.

When you are in alignment with your goals you are so inspired that you jump out of bed in the mornings and are motivated to work late. You become so purpose driven that it no longer seems like work, but just a natural extension of who you are.

Your life takes on a whole new meaning and you begin to operate in a whole new realm, which in turn enables you to live a life in harmony and flow. You begin to flow with the current as opposed to struggling upstream against it.

2. Handling Problems And Obstacles

As you begin to advance in the acquisition of your goals, it's only natural that you may encounter problems and obstacles. What is important to remember is that sometimes the challenge or problem you are facing may be the situation that enables you to make significant and successful leaps towards achieving your goals.

Your attitude and approach to handling your problems is what will make the difference in the results you will obtain in the end. In challenging times, keep your vision in front of you. Keep your eyes on the outcome! Know that these obstacles are just stepping-stones to getting you to where you need to be.

Problems and obstacles may only stop you permanently if you allow them to. When you are encountering a problem, see it as an opportunity to get a fresh perspective on things, or to re-strategize. Take some time off from your goals so you can rejuvenate and refocus in order to get back into a peak state.

3. Surround Yourself With Like-Minded People!

Keep yourself in an all time high. Surround yourself with like minded individuals and select the best friends and associates that truly like you and want to support you. It is such a beautiful thing to find people who genuinely would like to see you achieve your goals and become successful and happy. If you have those people in your life cherish them because they are few and hard to find.

Join success groups that are going to provide you with motivation and key tips on being successful. Invest in good books, CD's, and DVD's that teach you great life coaching, success, and other skills. They will add value to you as a person. Convert your car into a library and listen to positive and uplifting information as you drive.

Join professional associations of people in your field of business and career. This will help you to stay abreast of all the changes in your industry and provide you with a support group if needed. It can also foster harmony and goodwill and keep you motivated and allow you to have fun with it.

Operate with the mindset that this is the life that you are given and you're going to make the best of every situation that comes your way.

4. Draw On Your Past Confidence

Once you have begun to achieve success with your goals acknowledge that feeling of adjustment but draw on confidences of the past in order to be able to transition into the new role you are aspiring towards.

When you're down and out and cannot seem to find your motivation, draw on your past successes. Simply recollect all the past experiences when you were successful and relive those memories over and over again. Get totally engaged and awaken all the senses connected with those successful experiences.

Make a list of all the successful experiences you have had in the past and bask in the warmth of them all. Look at any certificates of achievement, trophies, business successes, community or volunteer committee successes and achievements.

If you do not have any past successes to draw on, then find ways to motivate yourself as discussed above. Listen to tapes and CDs of motivational speakers, read good books and find the right support group. Surround yourself with positive, nourishing, uplifting people who support and encourage your growth and applaud your successes.

5. Maintain Control Of Your Goals

As much as possible we must maintain control of our goals and the means to attaining them. This is a powerful concept and it makes a tremendous difference when we fully rely on our own abilities and strengths. The more control you hand over to others, the greater the possibility of being let down.

When your goal requires other people to make changes, this requirement places you in a vulnerable position and it may imply that you will not be able to get what you want unless you can get others to change first. Even though we may want things from and for other people, it is important that we formulate our goals in a way that will enable us to reach them independent of other people, since they are our goals and not someone else's.

Remember you can involve other people but you must be the one responsible for making critical decisions. The question to always ask yourself is "How can I take control of my current situation and make it what I would like it to be?"

For example if you were in a relationship and wanted to succeed in your profession but your partner does not want to give you the much needed support. Instead of setting out to change him or her (which may be near impossible or may take too much time and effort) what you should do is to open up yourself up to becoming more resourceful.

This could mean coming up with some creative ways to get around the situation or having a new perspective on what's needed. Being resourceful puts you in charge of your goals and places you in a more powerful position and resourceful state. I have seen too many people set out to try to change people or situations that were outside of their control, when instead they could have achieved their goals by focusing on implementing alternative strategies that could have yielded the same results.

Your Growth Process

Things don't always go the way we've planned. And there are times in life when achieving our goals, seems like a mountainous task. It may even appear as though you are taking one step forward and three backwards. Remember there is a learning curve and a growing process while attempting to acquire your goals. Your learning and growing is sometimes as important as achieving your goals. This would shape and mold you into the person you were meant to become, if your approach is the right one in those given circumstances.

Take this time to improve who you are, to develop the right mental and emotional fortitude. Seek personal, professional and spiritual advice in order to stay grounded. This is such as important strategy for success. It's the part that involves 100% of who you are and what you become in the process.

If you are currently practicing almost everything I have discussed and yet you cannot seem to manifest or gain the success you are looking for, do not despair. Sometimes you may have some learning and growing to do before you are ready to live in the fulfillment of that particular dream. Follow your gut and your instincts as you go along. Then give it some time – it will work out if it was meant to. Trust in an abundant, friendly universe. Continue to do your part and know that they will do theirs!

This is the one life that you know of so leave your mark and make a positive meaningful impact that outlasts your presence. Leaving your mark and creating an impact could be anything being the best manager, the best friend, a scientist who discovers a cure, a Mother Teresa, a Donald Trump, Queen

Rania and her humanitarian influence, a Lance Armstrong, a wonderful mom/dad, or the community doctor or business person? Why place limits on your accomplishments? After all this is your life!

We live in an abundant universe where anyone can fulfill their God given destiny. Just look around you and you will see ordinary people doing extraordinary feats with their lives. You will see others who seem to have very little yet who are able to have great accomplishments and live their dreams.

Believe that all things are possible, believe in yourself and believe that you are worthy. Keep your goals and desires in alignment with your life purpose.

You need not know every single step that it will take to achieve your goals – just decide what you want and start taking action on it.

CHAPTER 14

*If you have to lie, cheat and steal,
you're just not doing it right. My career is
a model of tough, fair dealings and fantastic
success without shortcuts, without breaking the law.*
Donald Trump

MOVING BEYOND TRADITIONAL STRATEGIES FOR SUCCESS

Some goals take years to accomplish and let's face it if it were that easy to attain then many people would have done it by now. You may have reached a point where you are facing some mental, emotional, financial, or support issues and challenges. People may be telling you to give it up because it's not worth it, but in your heart you know that it is. The outcome is far worth whatever you are currently experiencing.

In addition, for some of you, your outcome may be one that has far reaching consequences in the best interest of many and may ultimately change lives for the better or create a legacy for many generations to come and the continuous pursuit and success of this goal is critical.

If you are there then this chapter and the next are very important for you. It is time to begin to move beyond the standard practices of goal setting and into higher levels of goal attainment in the creation of the future you desire.

Having begun to work on your goals you need to continuously energize them, so that you can awaken and attract all the resources that you need in order to bring them to fruition.

In addition, you may need to implement strategies to keep yourself motivated and resourceful as you progress through your plan.

This level will require moving beyond traditional strategies for success. There are a great many levels of strategies that should be incorporated as you move up the various stages of your plan and obtain what it is you are aspiring to attain. It is only in this way that we can foster a world that is built on harmony for all its occupants and for generations to come!

Here are some further strategies that you can incorporate:

1. Energize Your Goals To Make Them Compelling And Attractive

The more powerful and inspiring our goals are, the more compelling our desire for us to achieve them. We must have something out there that's compelling enough to draw us forth and impel us to act and keep us motivated when faced with obstacles and challenges. Your dreams create an image of a future that you find motivating and this image builds the desire that is needed to go after achieving your goals!

In energizing our goals, we need to recognize that we process information through our different styles based on our senses: which are visual (seeing), auditory (hearing), kinesthetic (feeling), gustatory (taste), or olfactory (smell).

Although each of us uses all of our senses, we each have a preference for one or two more than the others. The preferred or dominant style should be the style you use when energizing your goals in order to create the motivation and drive that you are seeking. Your preference will influence the way that you interpret the world around you, how you understand others, and how you communicate including the words that you use.

For example, a person who is visual may find things more appealing when they actually see them. Therefore the best way for them to energize their goals or to stay motivated is by visualizing them!

Someone who is auditory should definitely repeat affirmations out loud in order to stay motivated, or listen to positive and motivational information.

Since we all filter and process information differently, it is highly effective to use techniques that best suits your style. *In fact, this is one of the critical factors in proper visualization, learning and self-motivation that many people are not aware of. In utilizing our dominant style to do any of these activities* we select would be the most appealing one to us and this will be the most effective style for keeping our goals energized and us highly motivated.

Engage all your senses when visualizing your goals. See each one clearly, and feel that satisfaction of having achieved it. They should be so real to us that they come alive in our imagination. We should be able to smell, taste, and feel our goals as though they were real and manifested. Make powerful statements and be aware of any feeling you may have.

As we practice the above exercise physiologically, this exercise should create the same stimulus response as if we already have the goal in our possession.

2. Employ Yourself At The Level Needed

Live your life with the intention of having realized its accomplishment. Take it to the next level and simply begin to live your life assuming the posture of someone who has what it takes to fulfill that role that what you want is already yours.

If you seek to achieve results in business, then you must expect to employ yourself at the level that is needed to attract all the success that you are expecting to achieve. By matching the frequency of what it is you are aspiring towards you will be more likely to attract it.

Create the consciousness that you need to fully accomplish your goals and fully assume the role! Providence will take over and before you know it, all kinds of wonderful things will begin to happen in your life.

It is worth mentioning that if you have not done the preparatory work and do not have what is needed to fulfill this role, then this method would be of no use to you. Simply go back to the essential building blocks of all that's needed to gain success and maintain it once you have received it. For example if your goal is to become a doctor and you have not done the necessary work or started to put things in place to gain success, then you are in fact wishing and not putting serious plans in place.

3. Know Your "Why" – Your Reasons For Pursuing Your Goals

One of the major reasons why people experience obstacles in staying motivated to achieve their goals is that there are not enough compelling reasons for them to persevere and follow through on their plan. When the going gets tough, their emotional highs begin to turn into emotional lows.

What are your reasons for wanting to achieve your goals and dreams? You are more likely to achieve your goals when they are connected to both a desire and a dream. Your goals are built on desires and what you truly want most in life. The stronger the desire, the more energy you will put into achieving it. Therefore, your desire in achieving those goals should be so strong that nothing can stand in your way.

Your "whys" are the deeper emotional reasons that drive those desires and create the "want" for wanting to achieve your goals. They are emotional drivers that fuel your fulfilling a lifelong dream or passion that you may have nurtured all your life.

We are drawn to whatever we find attractive and compelling. It consumes most of our waking moments and guides and directs our actions. Therefore, we must have compelling reasons to drive us forward to do whatever it takes to achieve our goals. And the way we do this is to focus on reasons that are bigger than our goals and even bigger than ourselves.

When we set goals, we are creating our destiny and shaping our life. Your "whys" should have the power to take you through tough times and give you the drive and resilience and dogged determination to achieve success in any situation. Your achievement of those goals is strongly dependent on the strength of your "whys".

For every goal you have written, state at least three reasons why you are committed to achieving them.

Leveraging The Power Of Pleasure And Pain

We are all motivated differently. Some people are motivated by what they have to lose (pain) and others by what they have to gain (pleasure). We must therefore leverage this principle in motivating ourselves for success. Your "why" should bring out emotions that provides both pleasure and pain - pleasure when you achieve your goals and pain when you have failed.

Imagine you have achieved your goals. Get into a solid state of knowing and look at the impact of having achieved your outcome on your life and those around you. Ask yourself:

- Why do I want to achieve my goals?

- Why am I doing this?

- What will I get out of it?

- What good will it really accomplish?

- Does it drive you emotionally?

- Does it create a positive impact to all concerned?

Your "Why" Should Be Bigger Than You

When you get inspired and are really excited about a goal, that inspiration should stimulate all the creativity that is needed to accomplish that goal. It is that simple, yet very powerful.

Here are some examples of Goals along with their intrinsic "Why"

Goal: Retire my wife.

Why/Reason: I love her and my kids very much and she would rather stay at home and take care of them and me. I am very hurt to see her unhappy every time she has go to work and drop the kids off at the day care.

Goal: Buying a home, or paying off a mortgage for a loved one, such as your parents.

Why/Reason: My parents have sacrificed throughout their lives to give myself and my brothers and sisters everything that we need. They never enjoyed a vacation or many of the things that they always wanted to do in order to pay bills and do whatever it took to ensure that all our needs were met. I want them to enjoy their life now that I am independent and in a position to reward them and do the same for them. It is an honor to repay them with happiness and pay off their mortgage.

Goal: Getting my dream vehicle.

Why/Reason: I love cars. They are one of my passions in life and are so beautifully made. After working hard and making a tremendous amount of sacrifice to accomplish so many successes in my life, my dream car is one of my gifts to myself. I have studied and worked hard to get where I am, I would like to treat myself to the vehicle of my dream.

Goal: Getting your dream home.

Why/Reason: My home is where I live and nurture myself, I have always dreamt of living in my dream home. My family and I would have so much pleasure in our dream home. It would make our lives so much more enjoyable.

Goals: Building schools in third world countries.

Why/Reason: I love kids. They are so innocent and dependant, yet in so many countries through no fault of theirs they lack basic amenities such as food, medical attention and shelter. They are our future generation and I would like to make a positive contribution to their lives. I believe that when we teach a man to fish, we feed him for life. I know that by educating children in third world countries I can give them an opportunity for a better life for themselves, their families and their countries and the world at large.

Discover Your Why

The goal itself does not provide you with any tangible reasons "why" you would like to accomplish it. Your "why" provides all the reasons and emotions that drives you to succeed!

Here are some questions to help you discover your reasons for pursuing your goals. Ask yourself:

Why do you want to achieve your (place name here) goals?

- Do you want to enhance your family tree?

- Do you want to elevate your status in life?

- Do you want to fulfill a lifelong dream?

- Are others depending on your success for their livelihood?

- Do you have a family to take care of?

- Have you been unable to fulfill the dreams of your loved ones?

- Is it out of a heart-felt gratitude for a selfless act from others or someone on your behalf?

- Are you continuously breaking promises to people that you love and want to start fulfilling them?

- Have you been disgusted with your job, life, or career and know that you must change it?

- Do you want to make a positive impact within your company?

- Do you want to make a contribution that would change society?

4. **Affirmations**

Affirmations are positive statements that describe a desired situation and act as motivating statements to spur you into action or to keep you going when the going gets tough. They are short, powerful, positive statements that enable you to have conscious control of your thoughts. When you say them, think them, or even hear them, they become the thoughts that help create your reality.

When used they are powerful tools that break through your limiting thoughts or beliefs and help to create new beneficial ones in line with the person you would like to become.

Research has shown that we have thousands of thoughts daily and the majority of these thoughts are negative. *When repeated often enough, affirmations replace limiting beliefs with more positive and empowering ones that can trigger us into positive action.* Affirmations enable you to be in conscious control of your thoughts.

I have heard some people criticize the use of affirmations through lack of proper understanding about what they are and how they are used and are beneficial to us. However, I firmly believe that when incorporated as part of your motivation strategy, affirmations can add power in your strategies for successful conditioning. They are useful tools to help change limiting belief, mental images, or negative thoughts that you hold about yourself. They are a great self-talk tool to boost your self-esteem and confidence.

Benefits of using affirmations:

- Since your thoughts and your words carry a vibration that is emitted and attracts what you are hoping for, you can create personal affirmations that can help reprogram your thinking.

- By consciously repeating affirmations, and seeing yourself at your best, you are able to be your best self-motivator.

Affirmations are one of the most powerful ways to bring you to the vibration match for what you want to attract in life.

- An affirmation propels you into action when you are facing challenges.

- Affirmations assist you to make immediate changes at an energetic level and if repeated enough times, transcends to your physical level.

- You can use affirmations to let the universe know that you are ready to start preparing yourself for what it is you would like to acquire in life.

- The use of affirmations will reaffirm all the positives about yourself in order to boost confidence and strengthen the qualities that you like.

How to write an affirmation:

- Clearly decide what it is you would like to affirm.

- Begin to write

- Be brief, specific and clear with your statement

- State exactly what it is you want.

- Use your preferred words and style in speaking.

- Keep your affirmation short.

- Use clear, positive and motivational words

- Keep your statement in the present. (When you write in the present tense, you are telling the universe that you are affirming the way you want it to be here and now. Not sometime in the future, but now.)

Here are some examples:

If your goal is to be happy, you could say:

> "I am absolutely happy and my happiness shines through in all that I do".

If your goal is to be a "positive influence" with people around you, you could say:

> "I am so happy and grateful that I am a positive influence to everyone I meet."

General Affirmations

- "I am a positive person".

- "I am blessed in all that I do".

- "I am vibrating at perfect health".

- "No matter what I eat I maintain a healthy body".

- "Success follows me where ever I go".

- "I attract and keep the perfect friends".

- "I am the perfection of God in me".

Tips when using affirmations:

- Affirmations can be said either verbally or mentally. My preferred choice is verbally in order to bring it into the physical realm.

- See yourself as the best of what you would like to become and then consciously and purposefully say your affirmations.

- Get an image or feeling of what you will be like, once you have achieved your outcome.

- To ensure their effectiveness, they should be repeated with attention, conviction, and desire.

- Be in a positive and happy state of gratitude and engage your emotions as you say and repeat them. Have fun when you are saying them and believe them as if they were absolutely true.

You Cannot Rely On Affirmations Alone

- You can use affirmations or affirmative phrases to help create change and make a new life for yourself, but you cannot rely on these words alone. Words without actions have no true meaning or power and they will not produce the results that you are after.

- Affirmations are useful in supporting your plans and actions that you are taking to achieve your goals, but cannot be a substitute for them.

- You can only make affirmations for yourself and not some other person; you should use words such as "I" or "Me" or use your name.

Awkwardness

When you have just begun to use affirmations you may feel awkward as you are making these statements as if you were telling a lie, but see it for what it is – a positive command to yourself and read back this section if needed. By filling your mind with the repetition of positive affirmations, you can begin to change your thought process and put an end to insecurity, doubt, or low self-esteem enabling yourself to release your talents and abilities.

5. Make Your Future Better Than The Past

Your past is filled with magnificent experiences that have brought you to this moment in time and made you into the person you are today. However, regardless of your past, tomorrow is a new day that brings with it a new canvass on which to paint a brand new life. Refocus, commit to your new goals and design the life that you were meant to live.

From now on, you can either live your life looking back with regrets, or you can take all your learning's and experiences from the past and use them as fuel for the future. Know that you are wiser and more prepared than ever to forge ahead. Let your dissatisfaction drive you to success. Build big dreams and challenge yourself for those dreams.

Make the future better than your past. Yesterday is gone and what we have is now is a gift and that is why they call it the "present."

Leave Yourself Open To Greater Outcomes

Expect to achieve and accomplish your goals - expect to win! Focus on the most and best that you want out of life. We live in a universe filled with abundance but life will give you whatever you ask of it and aim for - my personal philosophy is to aim for the stars and if you fall short you'll land on the clouds.

Never limit your expectations in all that you hope to achieve, dream bigger dreams and aim for the best. In asking for what you want, it is always best to always say (after you've asked for what you want) *"or if not this, then whatever is greater and in my highest interest and greatest good for my perfect well being!"*

Once you have said that, be open to the outcome, knowing that you have left the door open for an even bigger blessing to unfold in your life.

CHAPTER 15

*To trust in the force
that moves the universe is faith
Faith isn't blind, it's visionary.
Faith is believing that the universe
is on our side, and that the universe
knows what it is doing.
Author unknown*

TRUST IN A HIGHER POWER AND A POWERFULLY GOOD UNIVERSE

Let me begin by assuring you that I am not here to alter your beliefs in anyway – if, as you are reading this chapter the information resonates with you, then by all means use it! If on the other hand, it does not fit your style then that is perfectly fine.

I grew up acknowledging and believing in a divine power that is greater than us. Some call that divine power God or the Creator and others the Divine life force or loving universe. I believe that we are co-creators of our reality and that there is a benevolent spiritual being or beings who created and endowed us with divinity and all the power and abilities that we need in order to fulfill our destiny while here on earth.

We are all Divine children of the universe and each of us has a spiritual support team and system committed to making our life's journey easier and more successful, from the moment we're born to the moment we leave our physical bodies.

"Our Creator" or God and his/her powerful angels or guides, are with us to guide and protect us in truth, love and wisdom. As such it should be our goal to learn how to tap into the Divine Support System that is here to support us. Knowing this fact opens you up to amazing opportunities.

I know that when life gets tough this may be difficult to believe and we may feel as though we are alone and that we have to "tough" it out ourselves. But we do not have to.

When you ask for what you want and confidently put it out in the universe, amazing things can happen. You simply need to do your part, keep your heart open to receiving and trust knowing that it would be delivered to you.

Many Paths To Manifesting Your Goals

As you set your goals and may have even prepared your life plan, you do not need to know exactly how your goals will be manifested! There are many paths to your goals than you can ever imagine. Trust in your Divine Support System and leave yourself open to greater possibilities.

If you insist on controlling the manifestation of your goals, you are limiting the way in which your goals can come to you. Sometimes the way you have chosen may be long and painful, and there may be better ways of getting there. Once you have done your part, simply ask for what you want and end your request with:

"If not this, then give me something greater or for my greatest and highest good."

Then allow the outcome to happen! In doing we are able to prevent things that are not in our greater good, and open the door for an even bigger blessing or outcome! Sometimes we underestimate what we are capable of and demand less that we can receive from life.

Maximizing The Power Of Prayer And Setting Positive Outcomes

It's a good practice to commence every major activity with a positive intention, positive request and prayer. This is one of the most powerful ways to communicate and obtain guidance and assistance in all you're doing.

Through prayer or in our private moments of conversing with the Divine we should acknowledge and honor our Creator and the magnificent person he/she has created in us, since we are made in his/her own image. We should use our prayers to acknowledge all our blessings and accomplishments and all that we were created to become. We should also focus on all that we hope to accomplish in order to gain clarity and the strategies needed.

Some Benefits To Prayer

- Just like the Laws of Attraction, I believe that prayer is the power that enables you to tap into forces and connect to your divine life force (the very source from where you came). It enables you to access divine information to guide you to success in your personal request.

- Anytime you feel stuck or alone or sad, verbalize a prayer and release all that is holding you back.

- When we pray with sincerity and clear intentions and focus, we are able to stimulate creative ideas and send out vibrations that awaken and connect us with the force inherent in the spiritual universe. Prayer is a power-releasing, bondage-breaking activity that can help us produce the results we are looking for.

- We are all equipped with inner truth and an internal guidance system, and when we pray it is a wonderful way for us to gain clarity and receive the divine guidance we are seeking. When answers are revealed to us which can be through thoughts, people, situations and circumstances we should check our inner guidance to evaluate whether the answers we've received are consistent with our intuition.

- Prayer also provides quiet time for reflection and guidance in all that we do and gives us the chance to verbalize all our hurts, pains, fears and trials in situations where we find it difficult to talk to those around us. We are able to get things out of our system and free ourselves from that negativity.

- When you have set out to accomplish your goals and have done everything possible to make it work and may be facing many challenges and obstacles that seem insurmountable. You need to connect to your divine source and seek guidance in which move to make and what to do next.

There have been many occasions in life when I needed that divine help. There were times I felt stuck and I spoke a prayer that cleared up many things for me and enabled me to forge ahead supported by divine strength. The time I spent in prayer enabled me to get a better perspective and come up with unique solutions to my problems or sometimes, through divine intervention obstacles were removed.

A Positive Approach To Prayer

You can use a simple prayer as you would have a conversation with someone that you love and trust, such as a parent, best friend, or someone who loves you unconditionally.

A prayer could be a few simple words asking your Creator for help and guidance when you feel down, alone, afraid, heartbroken, ill, or any negativity that you are experiencing. It is our private moment when we can pour out our doubts, insecurities and fears without the fear of being judged or afraid for our privacy. Sometimes just being able to verbalize our fears, concerns, pains and hurts is very therapeutic and healing. It allows us this time to release any negativity and make way for more positive energies and solutions.

A prayer can also be a few simple words of gratitude and happiness for something good that happened to you or a magnificent feeling you are experiencing.

There are a multitude of reasons for praying or conversing with the Divine and here are a few:

- For the release of something negative.

- For requesting and receiving healing.

- Expressing feelings of gratitude for accomplishments, successes, good health etc.

- To keep yourself in a peak positive state.

- To seek guidance in business and personal issues.

- To be able to talk about things that are private and you may not be able to share with anyone else, such as guilt or burdens of your heart.

- For balance and overall peace, happiness and well-being.

- Connecting with your source and the divinity within.

There have been many scientific experiments done on the power of prayer where they were able to test the various positive physiological changes that occurred on and through people who were engaged in it. The positive energy that is created by prayer can create a positive impact on those around us through this positive vibration that is sent.

For those of you who may be interested, here is a formula that I have found to be very results-oriented in seeking guidance in life or in business:

- As best as you can **put yourself in a peak mental and emotional state** in order to emit positive vibration (I know that this may not always be possible, but a change in posture and physiology makes a big difference)

- If you are not in a peak state, choose a positive posture and positive words and continue to pray. If needed, release all your care to your Creator and then proceed to prayer.

- Say only what it is you want, focusing on the outcome that you want using simple and direct language

- Back up your prayer with visualization, positive thoughts and words

- Exercise gratitude and **be thankful** for all the positives in your life

- Do not only ask when you pray, but **affirm that you are receiving what is it you have prayed for** and be thankful for receiving it.

- Follow the methodology used in the Laws of Attraction when praying.

After You Have Prayed

Be in a state of receiving and allowing your desires to come to you. I have heard people continuously beg (not pray) for the same thing over and over as though the divine forces are not hearing. Act in a state of knowing that what you have prayed for will be accomplished in its proper time and that you not only can achieve it but have already received it. Remain in that state, giving thanks for having already received it until you have actually done so.

I believe that you can pray anywhere, as you are driving or doing your household choirs or simply enjoying some quiet time for yourself.

Sometimes there are no quick fixes to a particular problem or situation you are facing, or the answers you are seeking and it may take sometime to manifest the solutions you are looking for. Stay in a state of expectation and knowing that your request is being addressed.

As I have mentioned several times before, if your request is not being answered quickly enough, it is very important that you stay plugged into a positive group or circle of influence that can provide a positive buffer until you are better or have received the answers you are seeking.

Listen To Your Inner Messages/Intuition

As you pray, expect the messages and answers to be delivered to you. This is to take any form, it could be through friends, or situations in life or a feeling of knowing. Your Divine Source and Support team has a way of connecting with you and you will know when that happens (after all, this is where we came from and the system we are a part of).

I would like to mention here that there may be times when you may get a strong message that you should stop or change course while pursuing your goals, or get the answer to an issue you are facing. Always use your intuition and check the facts thoroughly and seek guidance if needed. Monitor all that you have accomplished to date and weigh everything properly before you decide. Somehow, by universal design the truth always seems to show up and is highlighted for all to see.

We must always practice good common and business sense and examine the advice received and evaluate the possible outcome before acting on it, carefully checking whether the advice received could cause us harm in any way. If you are undecided ask for clear guidance for the answers you are receiving and where applicable get professional advice from someone that you trust or an expert in that field.

It is important to note that we may not receive everything we ask. It could mean that what you are aspiring towards may not be the very best thing for you or in the best interest of others. For whatever reason, sometimes your goals may be off track and may interfere with your life's plan or that of someone else's. Ultimately, this may not be in your highest interest and could produce detrimental results in the long run.

In that situation the best outcome would be in not achieving your goals and not having achieved those goals could be a blessing in disguise!

Be thankful for the outcome and if you are not happy with it, ask for the wisdom of understanding in that situation so that you can learn, grow and understand the rationale for it.

Continue to live in gratitude, refocus, and set the intention to get back on your life's path.

Know that you are surrounded by a loving, ethical, friendly universe of justice, truth, universal love and light. And as we continue to do our best in all we do for this greater good, we will be protected, divinely guided and blessed with success and victory in all that we do.

CHAPTER 16

"Too often we underestimate the power of a touch, a smile, a kind word, a listening ear, an honest compliment, or the smallest act of caring, all of which have the potential to turn a life around."
Leo Buscaglia

CREATING THE ENVIRONMENT FOR SUCCESS

Your "Earth Luck" is based on the balance and harmony of what surrounds you. Being in harmony or disharmony with our environment can have either a positive or negative effect on the way we think and feel and as a result on our behavior.

As electromagnetic beings possessing our own unique electromagnetic energy system, we need to ensure that we are always operating in harmony with the environment around us.

"Earth Luck" leads to success. It is made up of our environmental influences such as our homes, working environments, and the cities and countries in which we live. Each of us occupies space on this earth that is in a particular geographical location in a particular hemisphere at specific magnetic points as indicated on a compass. All areas are different - not just climatically, but also energetically based on the influences of the seasons and are affected by the various planetary influences on that place. The dominant energies of a particular area can either deplete or enhance our own energies resulting in either a positive or negative impact in our lives.

This is not difficult for you to confirm. Simply look at the world around you and at the old system of things that is passing and observe various countries that are either at war or mired in poverty and look at the effects that these conditions both have on those nations. Did you know that a place contains a collective memory based on the collective energy and experiences of its people? When a place is in turmoil, whether through war, suffering or poverty - the mass consciousness created by that energy can blanket that area with negativity and affect everyone and their surroundings.

This is equally true for your home. Your home consists of an energy that is fuelled by the energy of the people and experiences occurring within that home. If you are happy and in harmony, that energy is transmitted throughout your home, creating a positive atmosphere. If on the other hand there is a great deal of anxiety or stress in a home this will also be reflected in the atmosphere.

If you have moved from one place to the other, you may have noticed significant changes in your life or your health. Every being occupies geographical space on this earth and each area is unique. Places come with their own individual climates and energies. As such, "Earth Luck" concerns our interaction with all the energies in the environment both outside and inside our homes and in any other places where we spend significant amounts of time.

Think about this –

- Have you ever been to a new place that put you on an "energy high" and made you feel happy and exhilarated?

- Conversely, have you ever been to a place where you felt drained of energy and uncomfortable and when you left that place you felt tired?

Electromagnetism

Scientifically, we are all electromagnetic beings surrounded by our unique force field, and we are living within in a larger electromagnetic field – the earth, and as a wider extension, our solar system and the entire universe.

On a smaller scale, the place or immediate environment that you live in will have either a positive or negative effect in your life. This includes our homes, towns, cities, or countries. When magnetic forces are in harmony with each other, (meaning that you are in correct alignment with the natural forces in your environment) your electrical impulses will become stronger and your energy and vibration levels will rise.

As a result of the positive effects your thoughts will get sharper, your body will heal more quickly, and your personal magnetism will rise to attract success, prosperity, romance, and happiness to you. Things will begin to go your way easily and naturally. The natural energy forces can boost the power of your electrical impulses while creating health and happiness for you.

On the other hand, if your magnetic forces are not in harmony with the natural forces in your environment, then your electrical impulses will get weaker and you will be out of alignment with the environment in which you are operating. This influence and lack of harmony with the magnetic forces can have negative repercussions in many aspects of your life, such as your health, success, and relationships! (For further research you can check my blog www.loanamorgan. wordpress.com for a list of some published materials on this subject.)

In simple terms, when your energy is low, chances are there was a clash in your magnetic field and those of your surroundings that affected your energy system. As a result your desire for success and the intensity of actions you take for success will also be low along with your motivation.

An example of this would be two magnets that repel versus two that attract. The harmonization of your magnetism with that of your environment causes many subtle changes in your mental, emotional, and physical state. These changes will be reflected in the results you produce through the fruits of your actions.

To emphasize the effects of this if you:

- are not having the desired level of success in the key areas of your life or

- are focused on your goals and would like to take action but just can't seem to get around to doing it or

- are finding it hard to succeed or

- keep encountering obstacles and/or health issues or

- have been doing everything right and have practiced all the right success strategies and techniques but are still not getting your desired results.

→ then you need to check your environment for imbalances and energy stealers.

Fortunately, this is relatively easy to do. You can start by simply spending conscious time in each area of your home in order to ascertain how you feel or what thought or images come to mind. As you go through your home or office - Do you feel inspired? Does your energy feel lifted? Do you feel happy and comfortable? Are you getting positive or negative images? If not, ask yourself, "What's missing?" or "What do I need to change, add or move around?"

You may intuitively know that you do not like a place but may not necessarily understand why. There may be a feeling or a thought or an image that lets you know if the energy of that place is positive or negative and if it enhances or depletes your well-being. Your intuition will guide you most of the times. You simply need to pay attention to the messages you are receiving, not only about your surroundings, but about your life in general.

Manipulating your environment for your success and as a result your earth luck and well being is within your control. You simply need to understand what contributes to it and the steps you can take to improve your surroundings. There are many factors that will contribute towards maximizing your Earth Luck. In this chapter, I have included a few that I consider to be important, easy to implement, and common to all of us.

Our Home

Various aspects of our lives are affected by the atmosphere of our home. One of the most important things that we can do is to establish a home that is joyful, comfortable and encouraging to those who dwell there: a place where family members can bond and revitalize physically, mentally and emotionally. A wonderful and happy surrounding sets the pace for success in every area of our lives. No matter where you live, you can create a home that will provide an environment that helps create health, prosperity, and happiness in all areas of your life.

Everything is comprised of energy and everything we own absorbs energy either from us, the people that we live with, our thoughts, intentions and feelings. The Chinese "energy masters" believe that the way we keep our home can either support or create obstacles to our success, happiness, good fortune, and health.

You can attract happiness and wealth with your spirit and mind, but if your home is not sending the universe the same message, it is difficult if not impossible for the universe to deliver. This is also applicable if there is disharmony around you. If there is then it is difficult if not impossible the universe bring you harmony because the message between your mind and your environment need to be in sync for manifestation to occur.

In order to attract harmony and success, your home should be an outer reflection of your desires and what it is you are hoping to attract. I certainly don't mean that you have to run out and invest in expensive furnishings or find a new home or embark on any major renovations. As you continue to read along, you will see what a fun and positive process this can be with very little investment on your part.

What Messages Are Your Surroundings Giving About You?

Our homes should not only reflect our personal tastes but also express the personalities of all who live there. Each room should be an extension of its occupant and provide an environment that facilitates success in every area of their life. It is the little things – colors, textures, patterns, wall coverings, plants, artwork, and the proper utilization of space - that makes the difference.

Your home or office acts as a conduit between what you create with your thoughts, feelings and actions and the world outside of you. What you surround yourself with is constantly giving unconscious messages to the Universe 24 hours a day; therefore every person should align their surrounding with all that they are aspiring towards.

This is your domain. This is your castle. If you want order and clarity in your life, then your home should reflect that. Do you have clutter lying around your home? Is everything neatly organized? Is your home clean and tidy? Does it have a pleasant smell? When you walk in, do you feel positive and energized? Listen to what the unconscious messages in your home are saying to you through its furnishings and other décor, such as photos and paintings. People tend to take their home atmosphere for granted or feel that it is too insignificant to make an important difference, but it makes quite a big impact on an energetic level.

What impressions do your surroundings convey about you? It's a good idea to close your eyes for a few minutes and then ask yourself:

"If I were a total stranger walking into my home, what impression does it give about me?"

- "What does it reflect?"
- "Does my home reflect all that I am aspiring to become?"
- "Does it reflect the love I am trying to foster in my family?"
- "Does it reflect the love I am trying to attract?"
- "Does it reflect the success I am or the success I am trying to attract?"
- "Does it reflect the wealth I am trying to attract?"
- "Does it reflect the happiness I would like in my life?"
- "Does it reflect peace and harmony?"
- "Does it foster great health or healing?"

Audit The Various Rooms In Your Home

Take a walk around your home. Start with the most intimate room – your bedroom. Look around and ask yourself, "Does my bedroom reflect everything I would like it to?" If you are married ask yourself, "Does my bedroom represent passion?" "Does it represent love and commitment?" "Does it reflect romance?"

Do the same exercise with appropriate questions in the other rooms in your home such as your study, office, family room, dining room, your children's room etc.

The paintings and other artwork in your home should support your goals and aspirations in the key areas of your life and that area of your home. Your children's room should contain posters and photos reflecting their goals, aspirations and mentors who have excelled in their field.

Your bedroom artwork should contain images of happily married couples, or convey love. Your living room should have images and artwork and paintings of positive, happy and vibrant images. Avoid putting images of violence in areas of rest, harmony and family etc.

Space Clearing

Create a healthy living space that lifts your energy and keeps you mentally, emotionally, and physically in harmony with your surroundings! This can be done by a simple cleaning and energizing in a variety of ways, such as positive or high energy music, spiritual music, scented candles, incense and rearranging your furniture to get rid of stagnant energy while creating and allowing the flow of new energy.

Remove All Clutter

Clutter comes in all forms. Clutter consists of items piled up around your home or office, or old clothing that has not been worn in years, and items just lying around the house that have not been used in a while.

Clutter also comes in the form of too many interior-decorating items around your home. In order to ensure a proper flow of energy that promotes a healthy sense of well-being, your surroundings should be balanced and properly laid out with thought and care.

Clearing clutter around you can assist in mental and emotional cleansing. In letting go of objects that you no longer use or may have negative memories that no longer serve you or you have outgrown, you are creating space for new energy that allows the universe to give you what you need.

We have all experienced the exhilarating feeling of walking into a clean home or environment where everything is neatly laid out and beautifully balanced. And we have also experienced the uneasiness of walking into an area that is dusty or cluttered with items that are piled up and thrown all over the place.

It is a great habit to remove all clutter from doorways and from any areas that block your walking path. I believe that at least once a year a person should invigorate their homes the way they would invigorate themselves.

Harmony and balance in your surroundings transfers to other areas of your life. Your home and office are where you spend most of your time and these areas should reflect the atmosphere for all you are aspiring towards.

Clearing Old Or Negative Energy To Make Way For The New

In order to welcome new energies into your life and to allow balance and a healthy energy flow, it is important that you engage in activities that will purge "old energy imprints" from your surroundings.

Try to air out your surroundings on a regular basis - open doors and windows to let new energy flow and sunlight into your home.

Set up images and photos of goals that you are aiming for - vacations, career success etc. You can find images in different types of magazines that can be strategically placed in your home. These items will keep you motivated and inspired when you look at them - especially in challenging times. It is also a good idea to change images and other interior decorating items around you to welcome positive changes and new energies into your life and home office.

Sometimes, years after a relationship has ended, I have seen people who kept photos and items from the past on display in their bedroom and other areas even when they wanted to move on and are looking for a new romance. How can they attract new energy, when they are still seeing images of those people around them? These images serve to trigger all the sad and negative emotions of the past experiences they represent.

Clear the old, and welcome the new.

Your Office

Your office is where you think, plan, hold meetings, conduct business, and strategize. Therefore, you need clarity around you when you think and work and in all your business dealings. Always make sure that your desk is clear and your papers are properly filed away.

Take a look at your surroundings in the office and ensure that it feels positive and is clutter free. Surround yourself with uplifting images that motivate you. As much as you can, have everything properly organized and professionally laid out. It is also a great idea to post work-related charts and goals on your wall to stimulate creativity and flow. Keep the energy dynamic and flowing by changing them on a regular basis to encourage positive changes and growth in business and your career.

Cleansing The Negative Energy Of A Geographical Area

In Ancient Times:

I remember reading about biblical events in ancient times where, when a city was facing a crisis the King would call for a period of fasting and prayer for his entire kingdom in order to clear the area of any negative influences. This collective focussed energy of the people was able to change the energy of a place and eventually that city would eradicate its crisis and gain victory over that situation.

In Our Modern World:

In our modern world people have learnt to use the "Laws of Attraction" and positive energy, focusing on the best of what they want in order to change a situation from negative to positive. *They know that as a people we can collectively feed the positive energy in this universe and create a world filled with love, healing, prosperity, empowerment, justice and integrity and enlightenment.*

They have also recognized that in order to welcome the new they have to cleanse the old. There are many magnificent groups that are focused on contributing to the greater good of everyone and to the world at large. They meet and collectively set positive intentions and pray about or meditate and send out powerful good intentions and vibrations, for the greater good of everyone, for world peace, healing and love to name a few.

How Can We Contribute To The Positive Energy?

We can all be a catalyst for the positive changes in our lives and in the world. Since our thoughts and words emit an electromagnetic influence - we need to focus on and speak about all the good we would like for ourselves, our future, our planet and our universe.

For example

- If it is perfect health that we have chosen to focus on achieving, then we need to focus on and speak only in terms of perfect health.

- If we would like peace then we must focus on and speak only about peace

- If we would like prosperity we need to focus on and speak only about prosperity.

By consciously feeding what is good, what is pure and what is true in this world, you will contribute to building the positive energy in this world and as a result, cleanse the negativity that exist in the magnetic field.

We can do this through prayers, meditation, positive thoughts, being happy and consciously sending out positive intentions for peace, prosperity, truth, love, joy and enlightenment into the universe.

As we focus on all the positives that we want and are able to navigate our lives in harmony with our focus we become more in control of our mental and emotional state and are able to consciously change any negative situations that arise to being the way we would like them to be.

As an added power boost for us, we should surround ourselves with related images, photos, music and like-minded people. This can be through our Vision Boards or many of the items that is discussed in chapter 17. Most importantly we need to actively speak wonderful things into our lives and into the world!

By this collective focus on all the goodness, healing and prosperity of this planet and our lives we are able to shift everything for the greater good for all of us and the generations to come.

Psychology Of Color And Your Environment

Color has significant impact on our lives and can affect our moods, health, well-being, and happiness. Colors are all around us and they are stimulating - not just to our senses but also to our energy level, our bodies, and our spirit. We can see it, feel it, and absorb it. Color definitely has an impact on our moods. Ask anyone and they will tell you at least two of their favorite colors.

Our bodies are stimulated and energized by some colors, and calmed and relaxed by others. Mentally and emotionally, color works on a deep level - changing our moods and affecting our sense of well being.

Spiritually, color is of immense significance. Employed in religious ritual throughout time, color is the language of the soul. From the saffron robes of Tibetan Buddhist monks and the royal blue of the Virgin Mary's cloak in

Christianity, to the black and white worn to represent, birth, death, or renewal. Colors have great symbolic power.

I could go into the science behind colors and their effect on human psychology and physiology, but for the sake of not boring you with too much detail, I suggest that if you would like more detailed information, you can easily find it by searching the internet.

Categorizing Colors

Warm colors include red, pink, orange, and yellow. These colors can evoke emotions ranging from feelings of warmth and comfort to feelings of anger and hostility. Warm colors energize the brain with positive energy. Warm colors fire us up and get us going.

Cool or calm colors include blue, purple, green, white, gray, and silver. At one end of the spectrum they are cold, impersonal, antiseptic colors. At the other end, the cool colors are comforting and nurturing.

So How Can You Manipulate Colors To Stimulate Happiness and Success?

Various ancient cultures, including the Egyptians, Indians, and Chinese used color for healing. Colors are particular wavelengths of electro-magnetic energy seen through our eyes and they affect our state of being.

The different hues and shades have direct subconscious effects on moods, energy levels and emotions. Therefore you should always be aware of the effects of colors on your emotions, your mood and your health and your loved ones.

The effects are easily seen with children. If your child is over energized or aggressive in nature, try changing the color of the child's room to a more calming color. Your home, your bedspread, and the clothes that you wear should be appealing and represent the mood you want to manifest. For example if your life is stressful, the healing power of color can help you relax and move into a more relaxed state. If you are ill or depressed there are certain colors that will lift your mood and put you in a more positive state.

If you want more passion in your romance or life, incorporate some energizing colors. If you want to lift your energy or mood, use a color that is relevant. If your energy or motivation is low, use warm colors to spice it up. In a nutshell, choose a color to stimulate the type of energy you are looking for.

It is important to note is that the effects of colors may vary from one person to another and may not necessarily be applicable to everyone. For example, what may energize one person may have the opposite effect on someone else. That is one of the reasons it is important to monitor your moods, emotions and health along with your long-term exposure to various colors.

The Energy and Messages Behind Colors

Red is a powerful color and has always been associated with vitality, passion and ambition. It can help overcome negative thoughts.

Orange is a warm, joyous color. It frees and releases emotions, stimulates the mind and renews interest in life. It is a wonderful anti-depressant and lifts the spirits.

Yellow is also a happy, bright, and uplifting color - a celebration of sunny days. It is associated with the intellectual side of the brain and stimulates our ability to think clearly and, makes decisions and assists our memory. It also helps us with good organization, with the assimilation of new ideas, and the ability to see different points of view. It builds self-confidence and encourages an optimistic attitude.

Green has a strong affinity with nature - helping us to connect and empathize with others and with the natural world. Green creates a feeling of comfort and relaxation, calmness and space, decreases stress, balances and soothes the emotions. It brings physical equilibrium and relaxation.

Deep blue is a cool, calming color. It represents the night, so it makes us feel calm and relaxed as if we are being soothed by the blue of the night sky. Light and soft blues makes us feel quiet and protected from the activities of the day.

Purple is a powerful psychic color associated with the right side of the brain, therefore stimulating intuition and imagination. Purple is also connected with artistic and musical impulses, mystery and sensitivity to beauty, and it stimulates creativity, inspiration, sensitivity, and spirituality.

White is the color of ultimate purity. It is an all around color of protection, bringing peace and comfort, alleviating emotional shock and despair, helping to cleanse our emotions, thought, and spirit. If you need time and space to reflect on your life, white can give you a feeling of freedom and uncluttered openness.

Black is associated with silence, the infinite, uncharted, and mysterious. Black can also prevent us from growing and changing. It is a grounding color and can be used as a cloak to hide from the world.

Gray is associated with independence, self-reliance, and self-control. Gray acts as a shield from outside influence. However, it generally has a negative feeling associated with fog, clouds, and cold. It is the color of evasion and non-commitment since it is neither black nor white.

Gold is associated with the sun and is therefore related to abundance and power, higher ideals, wisdom, and understanding. It is mentally revitalizing, energizing, and inspiring. It can also help to fight against fear and uncertainty.

Brown is the color of mother earth. Brown brings a sense of stability and alleviates insecurity.

Silver is the color of the moon, which is ever changing. It balances, harmonizes and is mentally cleansing.

Chinese Utilization Of Colors

In addition to the above, each color represents an element in Chinese interior decorating and energy practices as follows:

- blue and black signifies Water,
- silver, gray and white signifies Metal,
- yellow and brown signifies Earth,
- brown and green signifies Wood,
- red, orange and purple signifies Fire.

These elements signify and promote the energy of:

- Water - networking, communication, professional opportunities and wealth

- Wood - creative and innovative

- Metal - business and success

- Earth - stability, patience and balance

- Fire – energy, passion and enthusiasm

The colors in your home should be properly color coordinated to stimulate the energy you are trying to enhance or reduce or balance. Special attention should be placed on your bedroom and those of your children, since colors can affect the mood of a person.

The place where you live should be appealing to all your senses in order to stimulate your creativity and lift your mood.

WHAT WE MAKE OF OURSELVES – CREATING THE MASTERPIECE OF YOUR LIFE

In the words of the Buddha:
Do not believe in anything simply because you have heard it.
Do not believe in anything simply because it is spoken and rumored by many.
Do not believe in anything simply because it is
found written in your religious books.
Do not believe in anything merely on the authority of your teachers and elders.
Do not believe in traditions because they have been
handed down for many generations.
But after observation and analysis, when you find that
anything agrees with reason and is conducive to the good and
benefit of one and all, then accept it and live up to it.

CHAPTER 17

There is no competition; there is no end to the universal resources that fulfils these requests.
When you stay aligned with your energy stream, you always win, and somebody else does not have to lose for you to win. There is more than enough.
Esther & Jerry Hicks

ARE YOU HAPPY WITH WHAT YOU ARE ATTRACTING AND MANIFESTING

There are many times we may wonder if we are on the right track to getting all that we have set out to accomplish. Or if we are in the right state for attracting the success and happiness we desire. Here are two ways to know:

1. **Are You Achieving Your Outcome**

This is very straightforward and easy to measure, when you think about the various areas of your life. Are you accomplishing all that you have set out to accomplish? Are you attracting the right relationship or do you seem to attract the same questionable type of person all the time? Are you getting the results you are looking for in your professional pursuits, goals and aspiration? If you are, then great!

If not, try to evaluate why this may be happening. It may mean that you need to do something different. Work through the various exercises in this book and implement what you feel drawn to. Be flexible and then begin focusing ONLY on what you want.

2. Use Your Intuition and Feelings As A Guide

Trust your intuition as a guide especially if it's a continuous hunch or feeling. Your feelings and emotions are indicators regarding whether you are on the right track with your goals and objectives in the various areas of your life. They can act as an alert system if something may potentially cause you harm.

When you are feeling joy, peace or exhilaration it means you are on course and this can be an indicator that what you are focusing on and are engaged in are moving you closer to your life purpose and your current objectives.

On the other hand when you are feeling angry, sad or depressed or you have a nagging feeling of doubt or any other feeling that makes you uncomfortable then this is probably a warning that something is not right. Pay attention to those messages and check them against the results you are getting. If those feelings are in line with the results you're getting then act on your intuition and make whatever adjustments needed in order to get back on track.

Be In Control Of What You Are Attracting

There are many activities and practices to assist you to stay in control of what you are attracting. Here are some of the most important factors:

1. Set Clear Positive Outcomes

Being able to clearly decide what it is you want and then set your outcomes is one of the most important activities you can engage in. We have gone into details about this in our chapter on Goal Setting, please refer to it if needed.

2. Elevate Your Vibration

Most people tend to associate a feeling with a "vibe" (or vibration) and tend to use the word when they are describing how they feel about someone. For example we might say "I have a good vibe about her," or "there is something about him I do not like and I do not have a good vibe about him". A vibration is an energy frequency we emit and receive at different levels that affect our emotion at any given moment or time.

Although many people are aware of the positive or negative vibrations that they emit there are varying levels of vibration that have a direct influence on the various levels in the "elevation of mankind." There have been many scientific studies done on this area that have proven that humans who operate at very low levels of spiritual energy are also operating at low levels of awakened states of consciousness. And when operating at higher levels of vibration they begin to experience a more awakened state.

Each time you are experiencing a positive mood where you are happy, in love and at peace you send out a positive vibration. On the other hand if you are feeling angry, sad or resentful you emit a negative vibration. And you will attract more of the same.

A good example that illustrates this is like using a tuning fork. When you strike a tuning fork you activate it to send out a particular sound or frequency and in an area filled with tuning forks – only those that are tuned to the exact frequency will begin to vibrate in response. They will automatically connect and respond to the frequency that matches their own. So the key is to tune yourself to resonate at a frequency that is in harmony with what you want to attract.

It is imperative that you strive to keep your emotions in the positive range - feelings like joy, love, happiness, exhilaration, satisfaction, relief, pride, appreciation, relaxation and serenity. This will keep you on a high vibration level and allow you to attract higher frequencies for the best in life. When you are resonating at higher frequencies you will be able to enhance your personal power and become more empowered to create a life of success.

This is also one of the main reason why you must clearly decide what it is you want and the qualities around it and become that match it.

The higher the frequency the better the outcome in manifesting what you want. A higher frequency also provides the benefit of increasing your awareness and your connection with your Divine Source for the more superior outcome.

There are several ways that that you can raise your vibrations, they are the same techniques I have listed in the section above "The Magnetic Influence of Our Thoughts and Intentions". If these techniques are new to you it may take some time for you to master them. Then once you have gained greater control over your emotions, it will become easier for you to effortlessly release negative emotions when they arise. Make it a habit of having fun and focusing on all the positive aspects of life.

When you feel emotions fully and deeply, you radiate more intense frequencies into the universe. The stronger and more intense your feelings are, the more accelerated the process of vibrational attraction becomes. Think of the people you have encountered in your lifetime who seem to react positively to anything that comes their way, they are usually successful, because they refuse to allow negative experiences to control their activities.

Make it a habit to feel good every day. Do something that you really enjoy and participate in some activity that builds your energy and self esteem. Be happy and nurture your mind, body, spirit and soul.

3. Maximize The Power Of Prayer And Setting Positive Outcomes

Trust in a "Higher Power." Trust in a positive force that protects you and the universe. Some refer to that force as "Our Creator" and his/her powerful angels or guides, (our Divine Support System) positive benevolent beings that are with us to guide and protect us in truth, love and wisdom. Trust in that friendly universe! Know that there is a universal team is here to support you.

This is dealt with in greater detail in chapter # 15

4. Practice The Laws Of Attraction

As magnetic beings operating in this magnetic universe we are able to attract the various experiences in our lives through our dominant focus. We are subject to one of the most natural laws operating in the universe called the Laws of Attraction. Simply put it is defined as "I attract to my life whatever I give my attention, energy and focus to, whether positive or negative." In other words we will attract people, events, situations, ideas and thoughts that match our dominant thoughts, words, beliefs and feelings.

If you are focused on the good and positive behaviors, intentions and outcomes in your life, you will automatically attract more good and positive things into your life. On the other hand, if you are focused upon lack and negativity, then that is what will be attracted into your life.

This is dealt with in greater details in chapter #4

5. **Implement And Practice This Book**

There are many tested and proven "golden nuggets" of information throughout this book to guide and assist you in controlling what you would like to manifest. As you implement them and continue to gain mastery through repetitive use you will be in better control of what you are attracting.

6. **Be In A State Of Receiving**

To be in a state of receiving means that you have done all that is needed to accomplish your goals and visions, and as you proceed you operate with a feeling of expectancy and faith, knowing that you will accomplish all that you have set out to and your future is unfolding to provide the results you planned for.

To be in a state of receiving also means you are grateful and are expressing that gratitude for all that you have received and are currently enjoying in life. Be it friend and family members, financial success or health, no matter how trivial it may seem, always be thankful for what you have received. By operating at this feeling of gratitude you will be operating in a higher frequency and maintain a peak state to receive more. Make it a practice to be grateful for at least 5 things everyday. A statement that I learnt from Bob Proctor in the book "The Secret" is to begin by saying I am so happy and grateful for ..." and fill in what you are grateful about. Good energy always comes back ... especially through gratitude.

And finally in order to receive you need to believe that you are worthy of receiving all that you want. It is always a good idea to visualize yourself in that role and evaluate if it's a good fit. There are many reasons that can contribute to why someone may not feel unworthy to receive. They may have a low self-esteem; they may not be mentally, emotionally, physically of educationally trained and equipped for the results they are hoping for. And they may need to take the necessary steps to be better prepared, but may not have taken them yet or may be unwilling to pay the price necessary for the level of success they are aiming for.

Why You May Not Receive

People often wonder why it is they are practicing various goal-setting techniques and applying the "Laws of Attraction" and cannot seem to accomplish their goals or even if they do they never seem to reach the level they had hoped to acquire. There are many possible answers to that question but one has to remember that the Laws of Attraction is not "an absolute" guarantee or the "end-all." There are various factors that contribute to the various outcomes in our lives, but there are three in particular I would like to mention:

1. **Our God Given Destiny**

I believe that there are certain measures of events that are destined for us in this life. I certainly do not believe that we came aimlessly came into the world. We all have a plan and a purpose, and are all equipped with our God given talents and abilities.

When we are moving in line with this life purpose then we will acquire what is ours and as a result become truly fulfilled. There are many people searching and are unaware of their life's purpose and could end up making the wrong decisions. They may, for a number of reasons go after goals and dreams that are not consistent with their life path and as such, may try everything possible to acquire what they are hoping for yet may never get it. We must always be aware of our unique gifts and abilities and always be true to ourselves.

When something is right for you and you take all the right steps and implement the right techniques to acquire it then you will surely get it.

2. **If It Is Not In Your Highest Interest Or The Greater Good Of Everyone Concerned**

On a much higher level, everything that we do has far reaching consequences that we are sometimes unable to see at a particular moment. We live in a magnificent universe with so many divine forces guiding us in the decisions that we make. Not everything that we would like may be in our highest interest or for the greatest good of everyone concerned. The world is filled with examples of leaders or people who selfishly went after things that have brought harm to many and eventually resulted in their own demise.

Sometimes there is a blessing in not getting things that we go after, since there might be something greater than that for us. In many situations we not be aware of all the far reaching consequences or the domino effect out actions would take. We need to always operate with the purest intentions for all being that are being affected by all you do. I am sure many of you may have lost something that you really felt hurt and disappointed about, only to have something better come along later or to see in the wisdom in why you have lost it, as the years passed by.

3. Nothing Can Take The Place Of Hard Work And Preparation

I have seen too many people who believed they could simply use the Laws of Attraction and dream about their goals not exercising wisdom or implementing real techniques or taking the necessary action to achieve them. I have also met people who believed that if something is destined for them they do not have to work for it.

If you set a vision and a goal for yourself and use the Laws of Attraction *you will attract* what you are hoping for. However you may not be ready or equipped to handle that success when it comes. You must do all the necessary work and self development that is necessary to maximize opportunities when they come in order to fully utilize that success and be able to excel. You get prepared by having the right mental and emotional fortitude, learning, growing and developing the right training, skills, techniques and strategies that are needed in order to ensure that you achieve your goals.

A Few Platinum Universal Laws to Note:

"Never interfere with another's free will." Please do not set goals that include other people without their consent – this is a waste of your time and energy and it will not work. You might also find yourself going against the tide instead of flowing with it.

You are free to change whatever you would like in your own life, but never attempt to set intentions to change anyone else's life path. We are all on our own special journey and interfering with someone's life path is breaking one of the most significant laws in the universe.

As a simple example, asks any parent, couple, or company head, and they will tell you the outcome of trying to set plans for someone without their permission. If you would like to include people in your goals, please discuss it with them so that you can have their support before you proceed. This will save you a lot of wasted time, energy, and frustration.

There is definitely a reason why it is called free will. People have the right to choose without a third party imposing their own beliefs as to what is right for them.

We need to be mindful of this since the negative consequences of your past actions may be either blocking you or opening your life to success. There are also serious consequences in breaking this law.

You Are Here To Help Co-Create The World We Live In

You are here to help co-create the world around you and choose the magnificent life that you have always dreamed about, operating in a system where everyone around you is doing the same. We have to be mindful of what is being created at all times knowing that all that we choose to create will ultimately affect the greater whole. The more you begin to understand the power of the magnetic universe that we live in, the more you will understand how very important it is for you to take control of the results you want in your life.

You are creating a vibrational frequency with whatever you are giving your attention to – the thoughts you are thinking, the beliefs you are contemplating, the television show you are watching, the music you are listening to, the book you are reading, with whatever activity you are engaged in.

Focus only on what you truly want and on the perfect outcome for your life and goals. In that way your energies are channeled and focused towards the best; you are in control and you're in a better position to manifest what you want. Be a guide to yourself and others towards excellence but not necessarily perfection. And remember a core principle mentioned before - be flexible. "Always be open to greater or better than you may have planned for yourself."

CHAPTER 18

When one door closes
Another door opens
But we often look so long
and so regretfully upon the closed door
that we do not see the ones that are open for us
Alexander Graham Bell

RECLAIM YOUR PERSONAL POWER

Your personal power is a reflection of the creative, universal force within you. It is your personal power connecting with the Divine and the Source from which you came from. When it is developed and you are in touch with your personal power, you take responsibility for your life. You are focused and know what you need and want internally and are empowered from within to make your own choices and take the steps to fulfill your own needs. People who are in their personal power often empower rather than control others.

Everyone has personal power and is empowered with the freedom of personal choice, yet very few people live their lives from their place of power. Through lack of knowledge and awareness they have unknowingly given up their power to the various third party influences in their life and have developed a co-dependency on people, leaders, authorities and institutions that run their lives. They spend most of their lives making decisions based on others needs and wants instead of their own.

People give away their power when they make someone or something outside of themselves more important than what is inside of them. Since, they do not value who they are, they will seek to borrow their worth from the outer world and look for validation from people they believe know or have more than them. When you are able to let go of all external "entrapments", you are able to reconnect to who you are and your source.

When you reclaim your personal power, you build your self-confidence and self-esteem and as a result you are empowered to take control of your life and successfully go after your goals and create a better life for yourself. No one knows more about your path and purpose than yourself.

There are many ways that you can tell if you have given over your power to others:

- Do your relationships leave you feeling empty, less-than the person that you are or needy?

- Do you often follow the guidance of others, even though you don't really want to?

- Do you allow others to talk down or to, demean you?

- In certain relationships you feel manipulated or discounted?

- Do you give more than you receive in your relationships?

- Are you holding onto the anger and resentment about what happened to you in the past?

- Are you continuously critical of yourself?

- Are you giving more to your partner or spouse and they are not returning the same?

- Are you operating from a place of integrity in your relationship and they are not?

- Are you not being recognized for your contribution and taken advantage of in relationships or business?

- Are you refusing to forgive someone who has hurt and wronged you? (Refusing to forgive keeps you connected to that person and stuck in the past).

Here are some ways that you can maintain your position of personal power:

- Set boundaries

- Know how to stand up for your rights and beliefs
- Be able to set your own goals and stay focused
- Develop and trust your intuition
- Be able to say no
- Be your best friend
- Love yourself
- Build up your self-esteem
- Spend time on yourself and your dreams
- Recognize your self-worth
- Forgive and release any old hurts and move on without attachments.

Exercise:

- Make a list of all the ways that you give your personal power away.
- Listen to your self talk over the next couple of days and decide if you are your best friend or your worst critique. If you believe in the concept of a Divine Support team or God, then request that they guide you.
- Once you have developed your list, begin implementing strategies or changing your ways where applicable.
- Make a list of how you would like to be or react to situations in your life and then begin to incorporate it in your life.
- Knowing what I know now. What am I involved in today that I would not get involved in, if I had to do it all over again?

There are many factors that affect your personal power, but here are two major influential ones.

Social And Cultural Impact On Your Personal Power

Sometimes people cling to ideas and ideals from the various "influencers" in their lives. These are usually people of significance such as parents, teachers, religions leaders, friends and other loved ones, with whom they have spent a significant amount of time. In addition, to those, there are public figures such as political leaders and social trend influencers in the entertainment industry who create an impact in our lives.

In most instances their beliefs may be biased or based on untruths sent down through their tradition, cultures and beliefs. There may be biases of ancestral beliefs arising out of negative impacting experiences; that soon became an accepted belief among friends and family members. There are religious institutions and other groups that imposed their beliefs on their members.

Sometimes they may keep their members trapped in their dogmas and beliefs that are not in line with the "truth". Through these influences they have given up their personal power to these external bodies, and in doing so they are "led" and no longer think for themselves, and in the process no longer remember what it is they really want. They have been so conditioned over the years that *they need to cleanse themselves of all external conditioning and reclaim their power and authority in order to let go of the ideas of others and awaken to the true essence of who they are.* When they have done this, they are able to continue to grow and evolve to their highest interest as opposed to someone else's, or a group or some external force.

I once read where historically when a new Emperor took over a country after they have a won a battle and claimed the rights to governing a country, one of the very first acts they would perform is to destroy all the religions, cultural and historical records, literature and information of the previous regime. They would then proceed to impose their beliefs, traditions, religions and information in the country. This became part of their law and everything else was outlawed.

As a result some of the most influential books that have been used in religions and cultures are the results of this. Most of these books were filled with events of wars and power struggles for control of one nation over others.

Thank goodness, that is changing and we now live in a society that no longer accepts things because they have been passed on through generations nor traditions because they have been handed down from antiquity; nor rumors such as writings from supposed "great leaders or sages or religious leaders of the past. We have now moved into an age of enlightenment that has ushered in universal justice, healing, love, truth and compassion. We are now testing all teachings to ensure that they are in line with our consciousness and is in the best interest of all concerned. We are all children of God.

One of the most important exercise to release the things that hold you back in life or create disharmony or negativity is to let go of social and cultural beliefs and traditions that limits your beliefs about yourself and place undue demands and stress in your life. In doing so you will energetically cleanse your space and allow the right energy and experiences that you want in life.

What situations, people, groups and beliefs, exist in your life that no longer serves in your best interest or the higher interests of those around you? It may be time to start cleaning up your life in order to make room for the best you are capable of receiving.

As part of this process it is essential to filter out all the non-relevant things that were acquired throughout your life that no longer "serve your highest interest or greater good", and add no value to your purpose or have no significant impact on your happiness and fulfillment here on earth.

Let Go Of Social/Cultural Beliefs And Traditions That Should No Longer Be A Part Of Your Life.

Exercise: Ask yourself:

- What religious, cultural and social beliefs am I questioning that no longer make sense to me?

- Am I just going through the motions and following traditions and customs to please my family or the social circle that I live and operate in?

- What are my true beliefs about what I am hearing or reading? Is my better judgment and intuition telling me differently?

- What would I believe or practice if I had my freedom of choice? (because you do, you simply need to reclaim your personal power)

Let Go Of People/Relationships And Situations

We learn our lessons in life through people and situations, and no matter what we are experiencing there is always something to learn that can help us grow. But there are times when those situations and relationships have to come to an end. We need to know when to let go and move on and which relationship and situations that no longer make sense to be a part of especially when they are disempowering or negative and energy depleting. These could be any intimate, family or business relationships.

We may need to disconnect from those people and relationships such as friends, ex-lovers and spouses, business associates and extended family members. People who were a part of our past, but were only meant to be in our lives for a season or for a certain period of time and whose presence no longer serves us. They are no longer meant to be a part of our life and may act as a barrier to our God given destiny. Sometimes these are people that do no good, but only contribute to disharmony in our lives and make us unhappy and drained.

On the other hand, you may be experiencing the reverse where you may be the one that needs to move on. Some of the people in your life may have moved on and yet you may still be clinging to them either physically or emotionally. And by holding on to them you are not able to see the other people or situations in your life that offers a far greater level of happiness and fulfillment.

Here are some questions you can ask yourself:

- Am I happy with the people in my life?

- Are they living up to my expectations?

- Is this want I want for myself?

Lingering Energy Imprints From Relationships

When you have been in a long-term intimate relationship with someone energy connections are formed between you and them. Those energy connections can lead to creating lingering energy imprints from that relationship or situation. These energy imprints and connections are left on gifts and other intimate personal items that came out of that relationship – be it business or personal, but are especially strong in personal, intimate and physical contacts. Some people refer to this as "emotional baggage". **In order to clear your energetic field these imprints need to be cleared and released.**

Energy Occupies Space

Every situation and memory contains energy that occupies space in your life and in your energy field. What is essential to let go and clear your energy field and space and enjoy the benefit of available space that allows new energies to come into your life along with new experiences that bring joy and true fulfillment. In doing so, you will be able to enhance your energetic field and increase your personal magnetism.

If you do not clear out this old energy there are several unwanted things that may arise:

- You will continue to attract similar experiences to yourself

- With so little available clear space in your field it is difficult to allow new experiences to enter your life

- You would feel emotionally drained or sensitive to various issues

- There may be energy blockages that lead to various health issues

- Sometimes because that old energy exists, you may look for that person in everyone or continue to attract more of the same people in your life.

- By holding on to people, situations and things that no longer serve you, your energy is negatively spent and you are not free to truly attract what you really desire. This can lead to discouragement or a lack of motivation in other parts of your life.

Having old energetic influences is one of the major contributing factors why many people seem to get into the wrong romantic relationships over and over or attract the same types of people who haven't been good for them in the past. Or they may have the same kinds of experiences in business, and attract the same type of business partners.

Based on the Laws of Attraction we realize that without a new positive type of energy in line with what you want, you will continue to attract more of the same unwanted situations and people. Therefore in order to move ahead and create new opportunities for success you need:

1. to release what no longer serves you,

2. cleanse yourself

3. and then allow yourself to heal by enhancing your energy and acquiring the right energy for you to attract all that you want.

Here are some simple and effective exercises that you can engage in, in order to cleanse your field and attract the right type of energy into your life.

Cleansing Exercise – Cleanse Negativity From Your Relationship Field

1. List everything that you disliked in your last relationship(s), down to the minute detail

2. When you are done and have exhausted your list you can do one of two things:

    - Tear up the paper in pieces and throw it away or

    - Burn it,

3. As you are doing the above know that you have cleared that negative energy and made room for new positive relationships in your life.

4. Now that you have cleared the energies of the old, pull out your list of all that you want in a relationship and write down everything that you want in that person or relationship.

5. Energize the relationship goals you have written down as part of your goal setting exercise.

6. Begin celebrating and embracing your new beautiful, joyful, positive, loving and wholesome relationships that make you feel absolutely blessed and bring out the best in you!

Later on in the chapter "Create The Masterpiece Of Your Life". You will learn how you can energize all that you want through Vision Boards and Dream Books

Let Go Of The Other Person With Love

Always let go with love, integrity, compassion and gratitude. Honor the reasons for any relationship you have shared and are now ready to sever these ties. Be grateful for all the experiences shared and for the place where they have brought you today and appreciate their contribution to your growth. Honor yourself for having gone through the experience and in making this best decision with the resources and abilities you possess in that given situation

Honor the magnificence in their lives and in your own. Then move on to your greater destiny and the life that you truly desire and was meant for you.

Another A Simple Technique

Here is a very simple technique that you can use to begin cleansing your life:

Grab a pen and paper and begin writing down everything that has been an emotional strain or a bother to you. Keep writing and do not stop until you have written everything and feel as though you have drained all your negative emotions on that paper.

When you are finished crumple the paper and throw it away or burn it, with the clear intention that you are clearing away everything that needs to be removed from your life. As you have done this say the following:

"I honor myself in the highest frequency of love and light and for my higher purpose. I am grateful for all I have learned and the people who have shared my life until now. I take with me all my learning's, my growth and development to my next stage of my life and let go of everything that no longer serves me or my higher purpose."

Letting go of people, groups and associations that you love and have become attached to can be a rather difficult exercise for some. Many people tend to develop strong attachments to people or situation and may find it very challenging to let them go. Yet this is one of the most important and rewarding exercises you may ever go through in your life. There are times to recognize that some relationships cause you more pain and suffering than contributing to you as a person.

Note:

If you are uncertain or emotionally involved in a situation, you may need strength and support from people you can trust. In addition, there are situations you may need to heal and work on in key areas of yourself such as your self-esteem, self-love and confidence. Get into the right support group and honor yourself and take time to heal and strengthen. If needed, get second opinions or professional advice where needed for life changing decisions. Or if you are comfortable with your decision, then do what you know is right for you after considering all the factors involved.

CHAPTER 19

Something will master and something will serve.
Either you run the day or the day runs you;
either you run the business or the business runs you.
You must take personal responsibility
You cannot change the circumstances,
the seasons, or the wind, but you can
change yourself. That is something you
are in charge of.
Jim Rohn

MANAGING OUR TIME... MANAGING OUR LIFE!

Time Is Our Most Limited Resource

Everyday of our lives we are faced with numerous decisions and choices. And sometimes it is easier to choose things that give us momentary pleasures, but no real lasting value. Part of this is related to the fact that the "right choice" is often the difficult one – the one that involves short-term sacrifice of our pleasure.

In this fast paced life, with greater demands, increasing workloads and seemingly impossible deadlines, unless you are able to adopt efficient and effective time management techniques, you may end up stressed out, with very little time for personal use or room for growth in your personal, professional and spiritual life.

If you do not make your life, thoughts, goals and time a priority, you will be lost in the currents of other people's desires and expectations, tossing to and fro.

I have always lived my life from the perspective that in the end we are going to look back at our life and experience one of two emotions:

- Regret

Or

- Pride and divine peace knowing that we have accomplished what we had set out to do.

How you spend your time is important since time is the most precious and valuable asset that is given to us. It is perishable and irreplaceable and it cannot be saved. Therefore, what you choose to do with your time is critical to the quality and results you get out of life. Your time should be spent wisely on activities that bring the highest value to your life.

Most people are challenged to find productive or free time in their day which is crammed with a multitude of items that is near impossible to accomplish. One of the common reasons for this shortage of productive time is that people try to cram in activities and events that serve no real purpose in achieving their important, high-priority life, career, or business tasks and objectives.

Managing our life and our time is such as integral part of success and it starts with an inner decision that is manifested through our outer actions.

This chapter will not be the typical time management section that you can easily find in many books or on the internet. I am not going to have you go out and get a day planner or have you learn the features of any hand-held electronic device or the calendar on your computer. I am not going to ask you to meticulously cram your multitude of activities and events into any given day, week, month, or year.

Quite frankly, you can find that kind of information in any time-management book or article as there are quite a few amazing books written on the subject. There are many authors or trainers who have provided a tremendous number of techniques to help you effectively manage your time.

You can get ideas from them but you cannot do what everyone else does. Like most things in life, you have to do what works for you and fulfils your needs in managing your time since the demands on your time is different from other people.

What I am going to talk about is being able to develop your consciousness around managing yourself so that you can accomplish the major tasks and goals in your life.

The Importance Of Time Management

Regardless of your preferred style, the fact remains that in any given day, week, month, or year there are very important and significant things that we need to get done or face the consequences of not having achieved them. I am sure that you do not need to be reminded of the repercussions of missing a work task or school assignment or of forgetting a special occasion, meeting or event or business transaction. Probably everyone has experienced one of these unfortunate events and had to deal with a negative outcome or loss.

Preferred Style Of Time Management

There is no one way that is right for everyone and from experience I have observed that the most effective technique that you should implement is the one that you are drawn to and will provide the results you are looking for!

Time management is important and must be incorporated in some form or another. I know people who would meticulously plan almost every hour of everyday (including weekends) and always stay focused on their plan and that's great – it works for them. It simply means that this type of planning is their preferred style in doing things.

On the other hand, there are also people with no time management plans or documentation in their life who are happy operating that way. Achieving and remembering the things that need to get done is a hit or miss for them.

Then there are people who are somewhere in the middle. These are people who dislike meticulously planning and managing every hour of their time. People who enjoy spontaneity in life, but also recognize that there are multitudes of things that need to be accomplished so they do practice some form of time management.

Which Style Are You?

Do you use any form of time management in your life? How is it working for you? Are you able to accomplish all that you have set out to do or is there room for improvement? It is always a good idea to reflect on your past performance and evaluate whether you are accomplishing all the tasks that are important in any given period of time?

You should also look at all the goals you have established for your life in relation to the age by which you had hoped to accomplish them. If you are on track, excellent, give yourself a hug. On the other hand, while reflecting you realize that you are not on track, you need to evaluate what it is you are doing and seek better ways of accomplishing all that you have set out to.

Incorporate some effective techniques that will work for you based on your own personal style and preference. What is critical is for you to always be mindful of your time and set the intention to accomplish your goals and objectives on time.

Creating A Consciousness On Maximizing Your Time

Having recognized the importance of implementing some form of time management in life and the fact that not everyone has the same style, I went in search of one that is practical, achievable, and easy to implement.

What helped me the most was making a commitment to create a consciousness around maximizing my time. This is what I mean by this - we need to put ourselves in a state where we can easily recognize what is important to us at any given moment i.e. the things that will lead to the accomplishment of our overall goals and objectives.

At any time of the day there are multiple projects, reading materials, social and business events that are competing for our time. The reality is that the majority of these actually exists to fulfill someone else's desires and do not add value to our own goals and visions.

I am not referring to projects or activities that involve the key stakeholders in your life, such as your loved ones or employers/business associates or other significant people in your life. I am talking about people or events outside of your important external circle of influence. These could be people that drop by unannounced or without any real purpose in your office or your home.

It could also mean spending time reading or listening to information or engaging in activities that serves no relevant purpose in your life. This excludes the time that you have allocated for recreational purposes; since recreation should definitely be incorporated into your life as part of a balanced lifestyle.

We need to become aware of all the time wasters or stealers that we engage in that add no real value to our lives.

Once you have decided what is important in your life, the company you would like to keep and the goals and objectives you would like to pursue during your journey here on earth, we can now talk about some "overall life" time management skills and tips.

In doing the goal-achievement exercises set out in earlier chapters, managing your time is no longer something "abstract to you" but is real and has true relevance and meaning to your core focus in life.

It is my hope that you will have already gotten into a consciousness of what's important along with developing your abilities to set goals for yourself. It is my hope that you will have already gotten into a consciousness of what's important along with developing your abilities to set goals for yourself.

Now, when I discuss time management here, I am referring to the management of your life in relation to having ample focus and time for all that you consider to be of utmost importance to you. When you have a focus and a clear sense of direction, managing your time and your life will become second nature to you. It is as though there is a guiding force inside of you that navigates you toward all that is important in your life's vision. You instinctively know what to exclude and what to tolerate and include in your life. You have an innate sense of direction.

People With A Clear Sense Of Focus

All things being equal, what I have found is that people with a clear sense of focus are people you can look at and clearly see that "they know where they are going." They move through their life with a clear sense of direction. They always have a sense of purpose regarding what they are all about and where they are heading. When they steer off course or get sidetracked, they get back on course and stay firmly with their goals and purpose.

These people are usually able to effectively manage their time as a natural extension of their life even if their plans are not documented. They are people who naturally decline activities that are not driving them closer to where they need to be. They are proactive about their lives, and are unconsciously driven by their core goals and desires. Most of their time is spent working towards their goals and objectives and as a result things seem to fall into place. They have control of their lives and their destiny. They are in the driver's seat and they make things happen.

On the other hand, what I have realized is that when people seem to drift through life, most of the time it is because they lack a sense of purpose and direction and find themselves responding to life. Instead of being in control of their life, life tends to control them.

Time Management And Life Management Tips

I do acknowledge that even the best laid plans are sometimes affected by unexpected setbacks that can come out of the blue and throw us off course. It is during those times that we have to learn the art of simply allowing the setback that we are experiencing to pass until we get back on course. No matter what happens, stay firmly focused on what it is you hope to achieve and in the power and magnificence of who you are. Surround yourself with your loved ones and all that is beautiful and positive. Believe in yourself and in higher powers that love you and believe in you and it will be just a matter of time before you are back on target again - this time wiser and better prepared for all that lies ahead of you.

What is most important is that we learn from our experiences and setbacks. Once the timing is appropriate, we get right back onto your path - totally energized and empowered as someone who has learned and grown in areas that were needed to take us to the next level.

Here are some suggested broad-based, yet very strategic, time/life management tips that should help you accomplish some of most important things that you need to do at any given period of your life. These are tips that have helped me accomplish and manage some of the major goals and objectives I had set for myself.

1. **Spend Most Of Your Time Focused On Your Goals**

Our goals in the key areas of our life ranging from social, spiritual, recreational, family, career should always be our core focus when deciding how best to spend our time. Keep those goals firmly in front of you so they can act as a benchmark for how you spend your time.

At any given moment, you are faced with choices as to how you spend your time. You can choose to engage in activities that draw you closer to your goals, dreams, and aspirations or you could choose to spend time on trivial things that provide instant gratification but less added value to your overall goals and objectives. You can choose to watch television, or read a good book, or listen to uplifting CDs with relevant information that empower you to do something positive.

Overall, you have to be willing to do the things today that others won't do in order to have the things tomorrow that others won't have. And this calls for some up front sacrifices and discipline with how you allocated and spend your time. You will need to guard your time and be "selfish" in finding time for the most important activities in life.

Always maximize the use of time allocated on work and goal related activities. There should be balance in all we do. When you work – "work hard" and when you play – "play hard" and find the time to do all that is important. In order to maximize your time properly I recommend that whenever you are faced with items/activities that are vying for your time, make it a habit to ask yourself these questions:

- If I engage in this activity will it draw me any closer to achieving my goals?

- What value is this adding to me in any of the important areas of my life?

- What else could or should I be doing instead?

- How does this task support my higher goals and objectives?

2. **Maximize Your Pockets Of Spare Time**

Too many times I have seen people squander time with trivial activities inconsistent with their dreams and aspirations. It's hard to take action toward what you really want in life if you are too busy being involved in meaningless activities.

We all need a hobby or pastime and there is nothing wrong with doing those things – but to quote my dear uncle here – "too much of one thing is good for nothing".

This will call for up-front sacrifices and adjustments while remaining focused.

What will make a significant impact in achievement is how we spend our "in between time." We must always take control of and spend it wisely. As in the previous point made, this will also call for up-front sacrifices and adjustments in order to remain focused.

Your "in between time" is the various pockets of spare time you have through out your day. As an example, this could be the time spent on the subway or in your car trying to get to work. Sometimes these little pockets of time could add up to hours in a given day and a significant number of hours in a given week. For e.g. it might take you approximately 1 hour to an hour and a half getting to and from work. During that time you can listen to CDS and MP3s on personal or professional development. You can (if on the subway) engage in your studies or read books and materials to enhance your career or build your dreams.

At home or in the office during your 15 minutes pockets of time you can do some planning or brainstorming activities that are needed for some important task, or you can read or respond to emails or engage in some research for a project be in personal or professional.

3. **Take Regular Breaks**

Just as you have booked time off for important activities it is also important to book time for regular breaks. By taking regular breaks, you will stimulate your creativity and increase your energy level which in turn will increase your productivity.

This is especially applicable in situations where you are under time pressure and engaged in high stress activities. It's good to get up, move around and get some fresh air.

You will find that simply doing this may stimulate your creativity and enhance your ability to come up with some innovative ideas and remove any "stuck" emotions or blockages of ideas.

4. **Allocate Time For Important Activities and Events**

Allocate and book time for everything that is important in all aspects of your life including work, planning, "me time," socializing and romance, special occasions and down time. Give priority to the items that must be accomplished and also take time to simply "throw caution to wind" and engage in spontaneous activities for yourself or with friends or loved ones.

Take time to spend with family and loved ones. Organize fun events or romantic getaways. Do something adventurous and new and exciting. Have fancy dinners, book regular dates with your spouse. Book dates with your kids to spend quality time with them. Visit new places. Rejuvenate your mind, body, spirit and soul.

5. **Cultivate A To Do List**

Cultivate the habit of formulating a "to do" list every day in order for you to accomplish the important tasks that need to get done. Your to do list allows you the freedom to make any additional notes as needed.

Always separate the important from the urgent and allow the time for both. Prioritize the days /weeks activities. If you do not prioritize the day's activities, everything is of given equal importance, and you may overlook or not get to some very important items that need to get done.

When considering the importance of a task, decide whether it's among the top 10, 20 or 30 percent that creates the most value.

Once you have completed your list of what is important ask yourself the following:

- How important is this job/task? Does it need to be done now? Does it need to be done by me? Does it need to be done at all?

- What are the consequences of doing/not doing it?

- What is the most valuable use of my time right now?

Making short term sacrifices for the long-term gain is a critical key is the overall management of our life and our time.

6. **Identify All The "Time Wasters" And "Distracters"**

Just as important as finding ways to improve on your time it is very important that you evaluate and identify the time-wasters and distracters. It is also of utmost importance that you protect your quiet and productive time, by actually allocating and scheduling that time every day.

All through the day, we are faced with distractions that can range from answering the phone, to people who come into your office for idle gossip, to countless trivial emails, and other social media "noise", that may add no real value.

Cultivate the right habits for ignoring some of those distractions. Here are some things you can implement to help you maximize your time:

- Get into a mindset of clearly planning your day in advance

- Identify all your important and urgent tasks

- Utilize your most productive time to get the most important tasks completed

- Screen your calls and return less important calls at certain times during the day

- Focus on the task at hand; yet be flexible enough to multitask when needed. Where possible, block off and allocate time for each project

- When you work – work and when it's your leisure time – enjoy it.

- Find alternative ways to get things done in order to save time

- As much as you can develop agendas for your meetings and stick to it

- Delegate low priorities and low value tasks.

Diplomatically deal with some of your time-wasters, bearing in mind that your time is the most valuable, priceless, and limited asset in your life that should be spent wisely! Whenever possible, eliminate them and replace them with more important activities.

The world is dynamic and things can change in an instant and your priorities can change. Therefore, you should be always be prepared to be flexible and reassess your priorities, refocus your efforts and adjust your timelines when needed.

It is also important to recognize that there may be times when you may miss a deadline or find it difficult to juggle many priorities at the same time, please remember to be firm but kind to yourself. Simple make adjustments and stay on course.

CHAPTER 20

Recognize and accept that you are an important part of this beautiful world – you were wonderfully created by God and are keenly supported by your divine universal team. Any being as valuable and precious as you are would naturally be given all the resources needed to succeed.
Sonia Choquette

CREATE THE MASTERPIECE OF YOUR LIFE

Design Your Vision Board To Manifest Your Goals and Dreams

For decades, numerous studies have shown that writing down your goals is an extremely powerful method in achieving them. However, what is even more powerful is supporting those goals with pictures and beautiful affirmations! And two of my favorite ways of doing this, without a tremendous amount of thought and planning, and are fun to implement are Vision Boards and Dream Books.

What Is A "Vision Board"?

A "Vision Board" is a powerful visualization poster board that portrays your perfect life through the use of powerful intention statements and affirmations, supported by photos and other images of what you want. This is the "play book" of your life – your canvas on which you get to design the life you truly want and really have fun with – you are both the author and the artist. There are no limits to how you design your life through these Vision Boards.

The idea behind the Vision Board is that you are able to clearly and creatively document all that you want and surround yourself with images of who you would like to become. You can develop one for each area of your life reflecting the goals you are aspiring to accomplish in that area. You can set up one for the type of body and health you would like, the type of home you would like live in, places where you want to visit, your ideal love, your dream job etc.

In fact if you do not have time to sit down and focus on developing your goal achievement plan, but you know which goals you would like to pursue, then this such a magnificently engaging process of manifesting your goals without having to go through all the details of planning.

Be sure to have fun with it and approach it with a positive attitude. As you aspire to create the life that you are aiming for, creating harmony around you would make the journey more enjoyable. In developing a beautiful vision board that was creatively constructed with your goals, dreams and vision of your life, you are sending clear messages of what it is you want from the universe.

Why Set Up A "Vision Board"?

Every part of you and your creativity and senses are engaged when creating your board and as a result your life will change to match those images and desires through the Laws of Attraction and you will begin the process of manifesting your goals and dreams.

Sometimes you will discover that within a short time of setting it up things in your life will begin to take a positive turn for the best and doors to opportunities begin to present themselves to you.

Setting up a "Vision Board" is one of the most powerful visualization tools used for manifesting your goals and dreams. To me, it is one of the highest forms of "Goal Setting" since it engages all your senses and creativity. It is a beautiful display of all that you would like to have and accomplish in your life. It contains a written statement of what it is you want and the date to accomplish them by.

The Vision Board acts as a clear channel for the messages flowing between your mind and your environment and would synchronize them for manifestation to occur. When your mind and your environment are in sync, the universe will bring you harmony.

There are very few people who can boast of being able to diligently set aside time to sit down and focus on and document all their goals and dreams. The Vision Board is fun to prepare and can be prepared at anytime without a lot of major planning and fore thought and as a powerful tool that can be used in jump-starting your goal attainment process. These are your private moments when you seize control and paint a magnificent vision of what you would like your life to be.

It is so important to surround yourself with reminders and triggers to bring your focus back to what you want to attract. A Vision Board is a valuable tool used for setting your intentions and focusing on what you want.

In order to attract what we want - we need to focus our attention solely on it and ignore all that we do not want. Our days are consumed with a multitude of activities and thoughts that distract us from the things we are aspiring towards in life. What consumes our thoughts are the problems that we may be experiencing at any given time. It is sometimes impossible for us to continuously focus our thoughts on our goals and dreams. By properly setting up a Vision Board we are assured that for 24 hours a day, seven days a week we are sending out messages to the universe and energizing the vision of all that we want to manifest in our lives.

Types Of Vision Boards

There are different types of "Vision Boards" you can create a different one for each area of your life that you would like to focus on and your objectives and the outcomes you are seeking.

For example, you could set up a Vision Board for:

- Your Ideal Life - portraying the perfect outcome in all the major aspects of your life such as financial, career and family.

- Perfect Health or Perfect Body – portraying your idea of perfect health and the perfect body

- Romance – portraying your idea of the perfect, love, relationship, and partner. Energize it up with romantic and passionate images.

- Success and Prosperity – portraying your idea of success and wealth. Energize it up with images of things you would like to acquire.

- Your Dreams Board – portraying some, if not all of your life dreams

- Your Travel Board – portraying all the various cities and countries you would like to visit

- Your ideal business – portraying the perfect outcome of what you are aspiring towards in business.

Let us take your goal achievement plan to the next level and develop Vision Boards and Dreams Book to powerfully attract all that you are aspiring towards.

Vision Boards Are Not The Same For Everyone

Vision Boards should never be the same for everyone. We all have our unique blueprint and magnetic energy that we came into this world with. So that you can maximize the success patterns in your life!

In addition, we all have our unique tastes and preferences and our boards should reflect this when completed. The secret to quickly manifesting what you want is to understand the principles and techniques to follow while designing your Vision Board.

Tips When Creating Your Board

Have fun and be creative and listen to your intuition when creating your board. Whatever you do, trust that it is perfect and let your senses guide you. Be creative.

It is a great idea to place a photo of yourself in the middle and build your dreams around it.

Once you have decided on the perfect situation you are aiming for, then start collecting all the images and symbols you like that represent and support it. These can be photos of exactly what you would like to acquire, for example a particular vehicle, house or vacation spot. When your images are clear in your mind, it will be easy to find photos of them.

If you love various positive symbols then by all means use them. Some people love to use religious symbols and angels or religious leaders as part of their support team on their board. I know that kids love to draw colorful pictures - by all means let them be free in their expressions and do it.

Working on your board is an ongoing process and you should always leave space on your board for images or statements, etc. as you are inspired to. I have had situations in the past where I thought I had filled my Vision Boards with all that I loved and wanted, only to realize later that I left something out or I found a better image of what I would like to manifest.

Creating And Setting Up Your Vision Board

Since you have already decided on your wants and goals in Chapter 8, you can start creating "Vision Boards" for those now. Or, if you have something else in your heart that you would like to accomplish, then you can create a board in order to bring it into fruition and add life and energy to it.

Items you will need to set up a board:

- Foam board (my preferred choice, since they are nice and firm), Bristol boards or anything that you prefer to use as a base

- Magazines and photos with all the things that you would like to have such as:
    - images of people you are aspiring to be like,
    - all the material things you would like to possess,
    - all the places you would like to visit, the home you would like, the vehicle you would like to drive,
    - and the certificate and awards you would like to acquire.
    - You can also include images of the bank account balance you would like (you could use one of your existing bank statements and erase the current balance and simply type in the balance you would like.)
    - Use images, photos, intention statements and affirmations

- Glue stick

- Tape

- Markers, pens, colored pencils

Here is an example of how to set up your board:

Let's assume that you were setting up a board for success in business

- The first thing that you need to do before you start working on your Vision Board is to clearly identify what you want. Then write your perfect outcome statement for what it is you would like to accomplish. This will be used as your main theme that the board will be built around.

- You can place a photograph of yourself in the middle in order to surround yourself with all that you are aspiring towards.

- Now that your visions are clear, find photos and newspaper clippings that support all you are aspiring for. Get images of:

    - the ideal customers

    - $ value of checks you would like to receive

    - top business people in your field

    - buildings and other business related items you would like to own

    - magazine articles of business write-ups about your company

    - the vehicles you would be driving.

    - magazine clippings of the type of customers you would like to see in your business.

    - assets the business would like to own

- Write all kinds of positive and upbeat statements to support the life and business success you would like and place it in between the pictures on the board. Use some of the goals you have selected for yourself. Here are some of the things you could write:

- I attract my perfect customers

- The business generates an annual income of over $250,000 per annum.

- You may get bank statements and white out the amount written on it, and write in the amount of money you would like to see in your bank account.

- You can also find symbols that represent what you desire such as happiness, love and so on.

Have fun and create positive energy as you are working on your Vision Board. Play your favorite music and have a glass of wine or a nice cup of tea or your favorite drink as you are working on your board and building your dreams.

Whatever appeals to you, please go ahead and do it. Free your mind, become a kid again and have fun with everything.

It is a wonderful activity for couples to create a shared life Vision Board and some parents like to help their kids create one - I think that a Vision Board is great for fostering family relationships and bonding time. I highly recommend it.

Location For Your "Vision Board"

Ensure that you strategically place your board in your favorite location in your home. Some people have a preference for their bedroom or their office. Some people like to be private with their goals and dreams and place their board strategically away from visitors in their homes, while others are quite comfortable having them on display.

To fully utilize the Universal energy flowing in and around our homes and workplaces from all directions, the Vision Boards should be strategically placed to bring out the best results we are looking for! The Chinese use a great technique of placing the board in the best compass direction for success that suits your unique energetic field.

A Dream Book

In addition to, or as an alternative to Vision Boards you can build a Dream Book. A Dream Book is highly recommended for people who would like to keep their goals and dreams completely private or be able to work on and add to it as time progresses. In its creation, follow the same guidelines given above for Vision Boards, but instead of a board use a large notebook and utilize each page as your canvass.

Like the Vision Board the Dream Book is supported by the placement of beautiful photos, brochures, and other collages of images to help energize and add life to what it is you are "dreaming" about. These images will stimulate your creativity and help you to have fun and attract what it is you want

You can make it as elaborate or as simple as you would like it to be. In simple terms, it's your way of adding life to your dream.

For example, if you would like to go on a vacation to a five star resort in Mexico, write "My Mexican Vacation" on a blank page in your Dream Book. Get brochures of the resort you would like to stay in. Get pictures of all the places you would like to visit, such as restaurants and sites and also place them in the book. You can write some fun positive statements on the page.

If you would like to enter a triathlon, you can write "My Winning Triathlon Experience" in your Dream Book and get some photos (possibly from a magazine or from triatheletes that you may know) and place them on the page. Your statement can be written on the top of the page. You may also want to put some images of some of the best equipment you would use and medals that you would like to win. You might even put the time you would like to complete the event.

If you would like to own a particular car, write "My Dream Vehicle" and get a photo of the car and place it on the page. You can even go to the car dealer and sit in the vehicle and get a photograph of your self and place in in the book. And write some positive statements and put a date on it.

Since it is scientifically proven that we think in pictures, you can take your vision a bit further and add colors using creative add on to make your board more attractive.

Benefits Of A Dream Book

Here are some benefits of the Dream Book.

- It is useful if you have limited wall space or no privacy where you are living as, it provides the ideal solution. You can work on it and then put it safely away and whenever you need it you can take it out.

- Instead of using several boards, you can make different sections in the book for different areas of your life. And keep all your life aspirations in one book.

- Your dream book is private and enables you to do so much more, you can include your dreams and visions and add gratitude statements and continuously add to it as you go along.

- Whenever you want to view it, you simply take it out and go through all the pages, conduct your visioning exercises, and continue to build on it.

Using Affirmations

A very powerful way to energize and add life to your Vision Board and Dream Book is through the use of affirmations (covered in Chapter 14) and vision statements (covered in Chapter 7).

They can be placed directly on your Vision Board or in your Dream Book or you can write them on a piece of paper or index cards and attach them to your Vision Board. If they are very private and personal to you, you can put them in a sealed envelope and attach it either to the back or the front of the Board. In this way no one can read what you have written. You are free to place these statements on any part of the Board that you feel attracted to.

Unlike your life vision, it is a lot easier to write down your personal visions and aspirations for each area of your life. As such you can develop an individual vision statement for each area. You can do this by focusing on whatever you would like to manifest and personalize it to suit your needs - such as acquiring a new job, a relationship and so on.

CHAPTER 21

To Laugh often and much;
To win the respect of intelligent people and
the affection of children;
To earn the appreciation of honest critics
To appreciate beauty, to find the best in others
To leave the world a bit better,
whether by a healthy child, or garden patch
Or redeemed social condition;
To know even one life has breathed easier because you have lived
This is to have succeeded.
Ralph Waldo Emerson

WHAT WE MAKE OF OURSELVES

And now we have come to the end of this book and I hope that you were able to go through some if not all the information and exercises that you needed based on where you are at in your life. What I have found is that sometimes in reading a book there may be only a few key areas that we are drawn to. These are the areas that "bridge the gap" to what is missing for us at a particular time in our lives or with our goals and plans.

Our "Creator/God", has endowed us with great abilities and vast reserves of potential and our gift to "Him/Her" and to us is what we make of ourselves. When God gave us a dream - an unshakeable dream, know that we have been equipped with all the resources and abilities that we need to make that dream come true!

Success yesterday, today and tomorrow will always be the result of hard work. It is learning from our mistakes and perceived failures, maintaining a high level of integrity in all our dealings and showing loyalty to our company, business associates, friends and family members. It is dogged determination, combined with unrelenting efforts, until we have arrived at our chosen goals.

It is sometimes our difficult challenges that shape who we become in life. It is also important to note that, what our efforts make of us will always be of equal, if not far greater value, than what we will attain.

With the above in mind I would like to take this opportunity to share some words of wisdom with you as you continue along your quest for living an empowered life.

As You Continue To Succeed

As you continue to succeed and move to higher levels of success, it is important to go within yourself and raise your expectations about who you are and what you are capable of. Always challenge yourself to go beyond your present capabilities. Sometimes this may call for a complete restructuring of your habits and the beliefs you hold about yourself. Once you have come to the realization and understanding that what you make of your life is up to you, then you will be able to consciously design your life according to your own choices and desires.

There may be moments of self doubt when you may feel like quitting because things are just not going the way you had hoped. When you look at the accomplishments of others and think "there's no way I'll ever get there." It is at those times we need to stop, be flexible and take a new perspective and try new methods and strategies. There are several different ways to obtain your objectives.

What I learned is that the person you are comparing yourself to was right there in your shoes at some point in their life or career. But they recognized that success is a journey and part of their destiny. They had long-term vision and thinking and were able to move towards success with perseverance and focus in order to make their breakthrough.

The bigger the dreams, the bigger the challenges, and the greater the prize! Why the bigger the challenges you ask? Because you have to become more in order to achieve more – there are no ifs, ands, buts or maybes.

As you continue to pursue your dreams, be prepared for surprises and some obstacles along the way. Know that how you deal with any unexpected events will be the most important skill you will ever develop. Maintain a state of determination and self-belief, treating each situation as an opportunity to learn and become better and you will achieve success.

Take Responsibilities For Your Actions

Start taking responsibility for your thinking and actions and assume the attitude of a very astute student, knowing that in this journey of life we are here to learn and what we become is even greater than all we may materially achieve. We do not take our possessions with us when we leave this earth, we take all that we have learned and we leave behind all the good that we have accomplished and the deeds we have done. On a much deeper level and as eternal souls on our life's journey, what we make of ourselves is what would ultimately matter most, and will be our light that shines throughout this universe, even when we have left this earth. What we do today will have a powerful impact on everyone's tomorrows.

On the other hand, remember that the accumulation of physical assets and wealth are the fruits of our hard work: we have earned and deserve them and they should also be part of our aspirations. We live in a physical world and in order to enjoy life to the fullest we need financial prosperity. We must not only work hard or have philanthropic pursuits, but also find time to play and enjoy life to the max.

You should not only give but also be a receiver of all the richness that life has to offer. Enjoy every step of your journey and celebrate your successes every step of the way, no matter how small they may initially appear to be. Give yourself a big reward when you have accomplished any goal and when you have achieved success in any venture.

Your Legacy

What legacy will you leave behind when you leave this planet? What is your story going to be? Do you want to make a positive contribution to this planet? Are you going to change lives for the better? What are people going to say about you? How would you like to be remembered when you leave this earth?

Do you want to be remembered as the best dancer, or the best teacher or an amazing lover and best friend to your spouse, or as a very kind and strong person? Do you want to be remembered as a great parent or as a top-notch executive who made key strategic decisions that took your company to the next level and enhanced many lives? Do you want to be remembered for your great leadership or wonderful people skills? Whatever your answer, my advice to you is to *become that person now*!

There are too many people who are still waiting for that perfect moment and for all their "ducks to line up" before they start becoming that person or living the life that they have dreamed about! Then the months turn into years and before you know it, life is over and that perfect moment never came or it came and they may not have recognized it. That perfect moment is now for you to become that person you would like to be.

Always ask your Divine Support Team to give you unlimited alerts for that perfect moment. If you are ready for it - they would, or if not, they would help you to get to the next best alternative. Always remember that the goal is to aim for your perfect moment, since there may be far reaching consequences and like a domino effect could have repercussions on other events. And even in those times if things appear bleak or past the time, seek Divine guidance for your next steps and for help in assisting to rectify any negative repercussions.

Start walking in the direction of your goals and truly manifest your God given destiny. Your success will transcend money and all the material accumulations and move you into creating a lasting legacy and a name for yourself. In doing so you will be contributing to something that is far greater than you and adding to the greater good of this world and everyone in it.

Looking Back When We Get To The Top

When we get to the top of "Success Mountain" it is always important to remember where we came from and what it took to get there. Some people believe that "this is it" and get so caught up in the glamour of being at the top that they let the ball drop or they forgot the people that contributed to their success along the way. It is my belief that this is when our position requires us to be more responsible and use our power in a very ethical and empathetic manner.

Let your deeds and the person you've become outshine the money you've made and the material things you've accomplished. Be willing to help others along the way and "give back". As much as you can, render assistance to others in accomplishing their dreams. Remember that at some point in your life you needed help from someone else. You must also remember that you are not responsible for their hard work and what is needed in and from them to succeed. They have to take responsibility for doing what needs to get done and cannot depend on you to do everything.

We should definitely celebrate our successes along the way and treat ourselves to the very best of what we enjoy, striving for balance in all things by being both "selfless" and "self-focused" - Catering both to our needs and the needs of others.

Success is a journey and not a destination and whenever we believe that we have done it all, there is always something else that can be accomplished. Therefore we need to be flexible to change and open to new ideas and suggestions. Never ask or expect others to do what you would not do. Be a person of integrity and true to your word.

Be On the Lookout for Heroes

Throughout your life, always be on the lookout for heroes to admire and learn from and emulate. If you cannot find a hero, then become one and champion your cause. Be the change you wish to see. The world is in need of real leaders who will lead by example. No matter what our role is in this world, we are all leaders. Someone is always looking at us - our family members and our loved one, our friends, our kids, our co-workers, our employees, leaders, and other authority figures.

If there are admirable leaders in the areas you are looking for then that is excellent. If not, then what is even better is you becoming the leader that you are looking for! Remember we have our own destiny that we are blessed and ordained for.

The Law of Cause and Effect

There are laws that govern the universe and in whatever you do, be mindful of the potential far-reaching consequences and the effects on a global scale. Some call it the laws of "karma"; some call it the "law of cause and effect". The law state that for every action there is an equal and opposite reaction. Everything that we do affects someone. And whatever you sow comes back to you.

I have seen people who would do anything to gain success only to fail at other areas in their life. They did not consider the negative consequences their actions had on others. The world is filled with autobiographies of people who have had success at the expense of others. Let your life be different. Let your success be one that can be enjoyed - not only by yourself, but by everyone around you!

Being conscious that your actions will make this world a better place - not just for us but also for the future generation. It is not always easy to please everyone in all your actions and decisions. You can and do have an impact on everything from the success in your life to the world at large. Every thought and every deed that you perform will contribute towards it.

It is good practice to consider the implications of all your actions - both the positive and negative. After considering your actions, if you discovered that there are negative repercussions, then it is time to explore ways of making adjustments in order to have more of a positive impact.

Treat everyone with total respect because whatever you send out into the universe comes back and what goes around comes around. In other words adhere to the Golden Rule and "do unto others as you would have them do unto you". Therefore when you have achieved success, others will be happy to embrace your good fortune and love and admire your success because of the goodwill you exercised along your journey towards success, they will bless you with their thoughts, intentions and words.

Everyday Is A New Day

Recognize that you are the product of all your accumulated thoughts and actions up until this time. Recognize that you have the power and the ability to change your life. Every day is a new day. Each day brings with it new energies and a variety of choices. You can choose to make those choices that will make this the first day of the life you are seeking. Through exercising your free will, you have the power to use your God-given talents to make an enormous difference in your life and in the world.

Acknowledge that each new level of success that you have attained, brings with it new tasks, and new challenges, as well as amazing opportunities to rise to the next level!

As you continue to move on to "even higher levels" of achievement, *always* remember to incorporate all that you have learnt up until this moment in your life. By incorporating all that you have learnt, you are fully empowered to victoriously continue to climb the ladder of progress for your next steps of the journey.

Above all else, be true to yourself and be true to the truth that exists in your situation. Take all things into consideration and know that the truth is empowering and attached to freedom that truly lets your spirit soar.

Success is not only for a chosen few but for anyone willing to commit to what they want and make the necessary sacrifices. When you are able to reach your life goals and the visions you have for yourselves, you will serve as an example and give others permission to do the same in their lives.

You are given everything that you need to fulfill or rise above your life's mission! So be responsible and accountable for what you make of your life and be prepared for whatever comes your way. Know that you were born to soar high above mediocrity and towards greater levels of achievement.

I started off this book saying, *"There is no question about it "success and human luck" are created by many different factors - some obvious and some are unseen forces - and as a result one can't help but wonder if success is a combination of fate and free will."*

Now that I have come to the end of this book I hope that you are able to appreciate and understand that "yes" there are various factors that make up success and maybe some unseen forces are involved. But, with a clear vision for your life and clearly stated goals, backed by a well thought out plan, along with hard work, focus, dedication, and discipline you can attain your goals and be truly fulfilled and live your life purpose.

Never let the limits that others have placed on you be your benchmark for success. You are here to shape and create the best that you can ever envision for yourself. You are a child of the Divine and it is your Divine right to reign as a Prince or a Princess in this world. After all ... You Are Empowered For Success!

I honor the magnificence in you,
Sincerely,
Loana Morgan

ACKNOWLEDGEMENT

My first acknowledgement is to my Creator and my Divine Support Team, Universal Friends and myself. Thank you for the magnificence you have created with, in and around me. I would like to thank a loving and supportive Universe that has been with me on this magnificent journey of life. What an absolutely beautiful Universe we live in with such wonderful beings and creations of God!

I honor and thank:

… my beautiful Mom (Sumin) and my handsome Dad (Mohit) who has been such an inspiration and great teachers and inspiration in my life. You have always been such amazing support. Dad and mom you have given me so much strength and shared such wonderful wisdom with me. I absolutely love you both with all my heart and I honor you for being my parents. Thank you for your love and support always.

… my beautiful sister Lily. I simply cannot find the words to express all you have been to us growing up! You are my bestest bestest friend, sister and confidant and I love spending time with you. You are such a loving person filled with so much kindness, compassion and passion! You were my first cheerleader who believed in me! You are so much fun to be around and you have put up with all my moods. I love you so much.

… my brother Winston, my first teacher and party pal. You are so much fun to be around and such a support to all of us! You have continued to mature into such a magnificent big brother! Thank you for being such a wonderful support to all of us and reminding us with so much love, that your doors are always opened for us. I love you so much.

… my brother Kelvin. Growing up you have always been my buddy! We have had such great adventures (and fights lol) together! You have such a kind heart and have always been there for me. I love your passion for good food and music and good conversations in the car. I love you so much.

… my brother Amos (you are much more than a brother in law). You complete our family, being such an amazing brother to us all. Thanks for your love, guidance and support! You rock! I love our conversations over a nice glass of wine and some delicious international food. I love you very much.

… my sister Simone (much more than my sister in law) We've grown up together in so many ways (from JBs to Pleasure Island and from heartaches to laughter!) I have been part of and witnessed your blossoming into the independent essence of who you really are! I love you very much.

… my sister Marilyn (much more than my sister in law). You are definitely another big sister to all of us and you also complete our family. I love your contentment and humility. You are so kind and caring. I love you very much.

… wonderful Robin. You bring so much patience, love, wisdom and support to our family. Thank you for being such as amazing support to my brother. I love you very much.

… my nieces Candice, Renee, Lauren, Sarah, Shantal, Crystal, Amy, Gabrielle, Adriana, Tricia and my nephews Kaveet, Lawrence, Lance, Terrence, Gabriel and Luis. You guys are an absolute inspiration in my life. I am so blessed to have all of you in my life! You have all got such wonderful qualities that I love. I am so proud of you guys and I enjoy spending time with you and cherish every moment with you guys. Candice you have stepped up and are such an inspiration and role model to all your little sisters and cousins and so much fun to be around. I love you all very much!

… my cousin Neil and his wife Sharlene, you were such a support when I needed one! You rose to the occasion at a point in my life when I needed it the most. Words cannot express the gratitude that I feel. I love you guys very much.

… Vena and David and their beautiful kids Ananta, Tarran, and Devin. You guys have been my surrogate family. Thanks for including me as part of the family. I love you guys very much.

… My dear friend Sandra Ragbir. We met after so many years and you are such an inspiration to me. I am so proud of your ambition, drive and love for life. You affirmed to me what being empowered for success is all about. I love you very much!

… my late Grandmother Irene, Aunt Mogun, Uncle Lack, Mosie, Uncle Jattan.

… all my silent partners, teachers, coaches and authors who have inspired the greatness in me. I honor the magnificence in you! The Late Pastor Kenneth E Hagin, Sonia Choquette, Carolyn Myss, Marianne Williamson, Tom "Big Al" Schreiter, Jerry Clark, Nick Schestakov, Les Brown, Brian Tracy, Marie Diamond, Marcie Shimoff, Tony Robbins, Donald Trump, John Overdurf, Julie Silverthorn, Cheryl Richardson, Orin Daben, Sanaya Roman, Gregg Braden, Louise Hay, Dalai Lama, Lillian Too, Wauneen McMonagle, David Molden, Zig Ziglar, The Late Jim Rohn, The Founders of ACN – Mike and Tony Cupisz, Greg Provenzano and Robert Stevanovski. Larry Raskin, George Zalucki, Al and Jacqui Asensio.

… all the wonderful people who shared my life even for a few hours, 1 day, a few weeks, a few months or a few years and have made a contribution to the person I am today.

To my wonderful friends Dianna Rampersad, Lisa Ramkissoon, Colin Pinder, and Lola Adeniyi (my BFFs) who were the first readers of my book. Thanks for your insight and suggestions. I luv you guys very much!

To my absolutely wonderful independent editors:

Joanne Ray and June Fox. You are both amazing and so much more than Editors with your unique style and flare for editing. You've have been such support and poured out your heart into your editing of my book. Thank you for your suggestions, care, concern and attention to details. I honor the magnificence in both of you and I am blessed to have you as my editors.

PERMISSIONS:

I am grateful to the various individuals and organizations who have given me permission to reprint their material:

David Molden – Personal Development Trainer and Coach – www.quadrant1.com

Naomi Rhode – CPAE Speakers Hall of Fame, Author – www.jimrhode.com

The Feng Shui Society – www.FengShuiSociety.org.uk

Brian Tracy – Chairman and CEO of Brian Tracy International – www.briantracy.com